★ The War on Terrorism ★

LIFE OF AN AMERICAN SOLDIER IN AFGHANISTAN

AMERICAN WAR LIBRARY

★ **The War on Terrorism** ★

LIFE OF AN AMERICAN SOLDIER IN AFGHANISTAN

Titles in the American War Library series include:

The War on Terrorism
Combating the Global Terrorist Threat
Leaders and Generals
Life of an American Soldier in Afghanistan
The War at Home
The War in Afghanistan
Weapons of War

The American Revolution

The Civil War

The Cold War

The Korean War

The Persian Gulf War

The Vietnam War

World War I

World War II

AMERICAN
WAR LIBRARY

★ ★ ★ ★

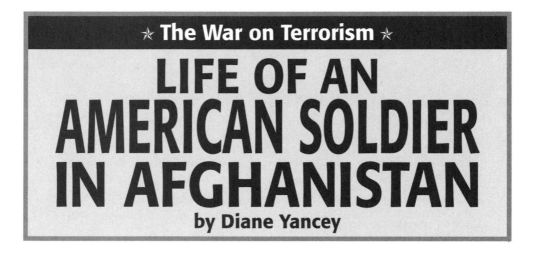

★ The War on Terrorism ★

LIFE OF AN AMERICAN SOLDIER IN AFGHANISTAN

by Diane Yancey

LUCENT
BOOKS ®

THOMSON

———— ✳ ————
™

GALE

San Diego • Detroit • New York • San Francisco • Cleveland • New Haven, Conn. • Waterville, Maine • London • Munich

THOMSON

GALE

© 2004 by Lucent Books. Lucent Books is an imprint of The Gale Group, Inc., a division of Thomson Learning, Inc.

Lucent Books® and Thomson Learning™ are trademarks used herein under license.

For more information, contact
Lucent Books
27500 Drake Rd.
Farmington Hills, MI 48331-3535
Or you can visit our Internet site at http://www.gale.com

LIBRARY OF CONGRESS CATALOGING-IN-PUBLICATION DATA

Yancey, Diane.
  Life of an American Soldier in Afghanistan / by Diane Yancey.
    v. cm.—(American war library; the war on terrorism)
  Includes bibliographical references and index.
  Contents: How soldiers cope?—Organizing for battle—Air attack over Afghanistan—Living conditions—Support personnel—Military life—Ground tactics.
    ISBN 1-59018-329-0 (hardback : alk. paper)
    1. United States—Juvenile literature. 2. War in Afghanistan, 2001—Equipment and supplies. [1. United States—Armed Forces—Soldiers. 2. War in Afghanistan, 2004-]
  I. Title. II. American war library. War on terrorism series.
    U750.Y56 2004
    956.7044'2373—dc21

Printed in the United States of America

★ Contents ★

A Nation Forged by War

The United States, like many nations, was forged and defined by war. Despite Benjamin Franklin's opinion that "There never was a good war or a bad peace," the United States owes its very existence to the War of Independence, one to which Franklin wholeheartedly subscribed. The country forged by war in 1776 was tempered and made stronger by the Civil War in the 1860s.

The Texas Revolution, the Mexican-American War, and the Spanish-American War expanded the country's borders and gave it overseas possessions. These wars made the United States a world power, but this status came with a price, as the nation became a key but reluctant player in both World War I and World War II.

Each successive war further defined the country's role on the world stage. Following World War II, U.S. foreign policy redefined itself to focus on the role of defender, not only of the freedom of its own citizens, but also of the freedom of people everywhere. During the Cold War that followed World War II until the collapse of the Soviet Union, defending the world meant fighting communism. This goal, manifested in the Korean and Vietnam conflicts, proved elusive, and soured the American public on its achievability. As the United States emerged as the world's sole superpower, American foreign policy has been guided less by national interest and more by protecting international human rights. But as involvement in Somalia and Kosovo prove, this goal has been equally elusive.

As a result, the country's view of itself changed. Bolstered by victories in World Wars I and II, Americans first relished the role of protector. But, as war followed war in a seemingly endless procession, Americans began to doubt their leaders, their motives, and themselves. The Vietnam War especially caused people to question the validity of sending its young people to die in places where they were not particularly wanted and for people who did not seem especially grateful.

While the most obvious changes brought about by America's wars have been geopolitical in nature, many other aspects of society have been touched. War often does not bring about change directly, but acts instead like the catalyst in a chemical reaction, accelerating changes already in progress.

Some of these changes have been societal. The role of women in the United States had been slowly changing, but World War II put thousands into the workforce and into uniform. They might have gone back to being housewives after the war, but equality, once experienced, would not be forgotten.

Likewise, wars have accelerated technological change. The necessity for faster airplanes and more destructive bombs led to the development of jet planes and nuclear energy. Artificial fibers developed for parachutes in the 1940s were used in clothing of the 1950s.

Lucent Books' American War Library covers key wars in the development of the nation. Each war is covered in several volumes, to allow for more detail, context, and to provide volumes on often neglected subjects, such as the kamikazes of World War II, or the weapons used in the Civil War. As with all Lucent books, notes, annotated bibliographies, and appendixes such as glossaries give students a launching point for further research. In addition, sidebars and archival photographs enhance the text. Together, each volume in the American War Library will aid students in understanding how America's wars have shaped and changed its politics, economics, and society.

"A Certain Force in an Uncertain World"

September 11, 2001, dawned in an ordinary way for most Americans. On the East Coast, sunshine and blue skies promised a pleasant day. Children prepared for school. Adults set off for work. Keith Winchell, a city police officer and an air force reservist, was getting ready for his usual tough shift on patrol. "I work in the Bronx. I get bottles thrown at me from rooftops,"[1] he says, describing his job.

At 8:45 A.M. eastern standard time, however, everyone's daily routine was turned upside down. At that moment, a fully loaded aircraft, American Airlines Flight 11 out of Boston, Massachusetts, crashed into the north tower of the World Trade Center in New York City, tearing an enormous hole in the building and setting it afire. Less than twenty minutes later, a second plane, United Airlines Flight 175 from Boston, crashed into the south tower of the center and exploded. "When the first plane hit the World Trade Center, you thought it was a tragic accident," remembers army sergeant Tony Vets, who was on leave in Louisiana and watched the disaster on television. "But as the events unfolded, it was obvious to everyone that it was a planned attack."[2]

As the two towers burned and then collapsed, news anchors reported the unthinkable. A third plane—American Airlines Flight 77—had crashed into the Pentagon, and a fourth—United Airlines Flight 93—had nose-dived into the Pennsylvania countryside, southeast of Pittsburgh. Everyone onboard the airliners had been killed. Thousands in the twin towers and more than one hundred people in the Pentagon died as well.

In shock and horror, Americans sat glued to their television sets for hours on end, listening to details of the tragedy. When a realization of the extent of the destruction set in, millions of people did what they could to help, donating money, blood, goods, and time to the recovery effort. People from every walk of life came together

The terrorist attacks on the World Trade Center towers shocked most Americans.

to mourn for those who were lost. Winchell, and thousands of others, spent weeks at Ground Zero (the New York City crash site), determined to find survivors and the bodies of the dead. The work was emotionally and physically draining, and it was an undertaking that none of them would ever forget. "I've seen the devastation," Winchell says. "I had to carry caskets of some of my friends."[3]

Assigning the Blame

As the nation mourned, experts quickly determined that the attacks had been planned and carried out by al-Qaeda, a radical Islamic organization headed by Saudi-born terrorist Osama bin Laden. The hijackers had left letters and documents behind attesting to their connection with the organization.

Al-Qaeda, whose goal it was to carry out bin Laden's terrorist plans, had targeted Americans several times before, but never with such damaging effect. In February 1993, a bomb exploded in the parking garage of the World Trade Center, killing six people and injuring more than one thousand. In October 1993, al-Qaeda attacks against U.S. Army personnel in Mogadishu, Somalia, resulted in the deaths of eighteen soldiers. A June 1996 bomb attack in Saudi Arabia killed nineteen Americans, while the bombings of U.S. embassies in Kenya and Tanzania in August 1998 resulted in more than 250 deaths. Finally, on October 12, 2000, an explosive-packed boat rammed the navy destroyer USS *Cole* during a refueling stop in Aden, Yemen, killing seventeen sailors, wounding thirty-nine, and leaving the billion-dollar warship crippled.

Bin Laden, who had become an international fugitive because of his terrorist activities, chose the country of Afghanistan as a hiding place and had been undercover there since 1996. The country was the perfect setting for his terrorist operation. Many portions of the land were wild and unpopulated. Social systems had been destroyed or impaired by a decade of war with the Soviet Union and additional years of civil strife between Afghan warlords. The Taliban, a group of repressive fundamentalist Muslims, had seized political power in 1995 and were sympathetic to bin Laden's cause. They provided shelter and support for him and his associates.

"We Have to Go After Them"

On September 12, 2001, President George W. Bush declared war on terrorism and vowed that the United States would defeat bin Laden, members of al-Qaeda, and any

Attacks That Changed Our World

Brigadier General James A. Marks was preparing to take command of the U.S. Army Intelligence Center at Fort Huachuca, Arizona, on September 11, 2001. An account of his reaction when he received news of the terrorist attacks in New York City and Washington, D.C., was published in the July–September 2002 issue of the *Military Intelligence Professional Bulletin*.

I was in the guesthouse and, like every soldier, was polishing my boots and squaring away my uniform when my daughter called me to the television. My jaw nearly hit the floor. The top floors of one of the World Trade Center buildings was a mass of black smoke and flame. The initial reports were somewhat confusing. An aircraft, believed to be a passenger jet, had apparently slammed into the building. It was a clear, bright morning in New York and I wrestled to grasp how such a collision could occur. I could only think this was no accident. This was a deliberate attack. I followed the flight of the second jet. . . . There were no doubts now, our country was under attack. . . .

There was, however, little time for reflection. . . . I had a job to do. There were soldiers in formation who awoke that morning to a country at peace and within the span of twenty minutes, found her at war. . . . Those twenty minutes between the first and last suicide attacks had forever changed their world.

other group or government that sponsored terrorism. "People who [threaten and kill Americans] are our enemies, and people who support those people will also be treated as our enemies,"[4] stated a high ranking U.S. official that year.

When the Taliban government refused to capture and turn over bin Laden, Afghanistan became the setting for the first chapter of the war on terrorism. Americans like Keith Winchell, who had been deeply disturbed by the September attacks and feared similar assaults in the future, sup-

ported the move to war wholeheartedly. "The terrorists are criminals," he pointed out. "They just killed more than the average criminal does. They committed the crime, so we have to go after them."[5]

Many military personnel were not surprised that the attacks on September 11 led to a war with terrorists. In fact, as soon as seasoned veterans saw the second plane crash into the World Trade Center, they ex-

The day after the September 11 attacks, President Bush declared war on terrorism.

"Surrender Now"

Shortly after declaring war against the Taliban, nations led by the United States dropped several different types of informational flyers titled "The Partnership of Nations Is Here to Help" over Afghanistan. A portion of one, which urged the Taliban to surrender, is included below and can be read in its entirety on the Internet at www.cnn.com.

Attention Taliban! You are condemned. The instant the terrorists you support took over our planes, you sentenced yourselves to death. The Armed Forces of the United States are here to seek justice for our dead.

Highly trained soldiers are coming to shut down once and for all Usama bin Laden's ring of terrorism, and the Taliban that supports them and their actions. . . .

You have only one choice. . . . Surrender now and we will give you a second chance. We will let you live. If you surrender no harm will come to you. When you decide to surrender, approach United States forces with your hands in the air. Sling your weapon across you back muzzle towards the ground. Remove your magazine and expel any rounds. Doing this is your only chance of survival.

pected the announcement. "It [was] a night none of us will forget," remembers U.S. Army captain Jason Amerine, who was stationed with his detachment in the Republic of Kazakhstan, south of Russia, when he got word of the attacks. "We talked over what we expected would happen next. What we anticipated was that this meant a war had just started. We didn't exactly know where, although, even at that point, all of us had a pretty good idea of where it would be centered . . . Afghanistan."[6]

Taking Care of Business

Amerine was correct. Within an hour of the attacks, commanders at the Pentagon had begun planning a response. And, as the word went out that military action would begin in Afghanistan, thousands of U.S. military personnel began preparing to go overseas, to face danger and loneli-

ness, and to be, as a U.S marine motto attested, "a certain force in an uncertain world."[7]

Those who were called to war quickly learned that the conflict would be a difficult one. The enemy was elusive. The goals would be difficult to achieve. Life in Afghanistan was a grueling experience that few participants would ever forget. Nevertheless, all were willing to accept the assignment and get on with the work. "When you're in the chow hall, you overhear people talking. People are saying, 'let's go.' I don't know who they are, but people want to end this, right now," said Army specialist Michael Huddleston, who put the spirit of the military into words. "We are here so that America can go to bed at night. They can rest knowing that we are here to protect them if anything happens. And that's what I've always wanted to do."[8]

Chapter 1

War in a Far-Off Land

Despite earlier terrorist attacks on U.S. targets throughout the world, few Americans—military personnel or civilians—foresaw that their country would be going to war in Afghanistan in the last months of 2001. Faced with that war, however, most realized that their knowledge of that nation was extremely limited, based on sketchy information supplied by news reporters who had covered the Soviet-Afghan War of the 1980s. They needed and wanted more particulars. As authors Philip Cheng and Laurie McBean wrote in an article for *Earth Observation Magazine:*

> In the days following those attacks [of September 11], many people, organizations and news agencies began looking for recent images, maps, and any other information on Afghanistan. Questions were immediately raised that included, "Where is Afghanistan, and where are its major population centers?" "What has happened in Afghanistan over the past decade?" "What is the geography of Afghanistan and how does its terrain affect its economy and its citizens?"[9]

The Theater

As Americans began to learn about Afghanistan, they discovered that it was extremely different from the United States with its prosperity, diversity, and Western values. Afghanistan is a landlocked Asian nation, slightly smaller than Texas, and made up primarily of mountains and deserts. The weather is usually dry, with hot summers and cold winters. The people, among the poorest and least educated in the world, are Muslim tribesmen who were loyal primarily to their own ethnic group. Pashtuns are a majority in the country, with Hazaras, Tajiks, and Uzbeks being significant minorities. With few contacts with the outside world, most Afghans wanted little more than peace and security for themselves and their families.

Americans took such conditions for granted, but they remained merely a dream in Afghanistan, especially during the 1980s. During that time, the Communist-controlled Soviet Union, anxious to expand its sphere of influence around the world, attempted a takeover of its Muslim-dominated neighbor to the south. Afghanistan's government had been pro-Soviet since the overthrow of King Zahir Shah in 1973, but its people had a strong dislike of outsiders trying to occupy their country. They organized to expel the Soviet invaders.

For ten years, many of the bravest Afghan men, known as mujahideen, or holy warriors, fought tirelessly to that end against almost impossible odds. They did so with the covert aid of allies like Saudi Arabia and the United States, who supplied them with money and modern weapons. That aid, coupled with their determination, was enough to thwart the enemy. In 1989, the Soviet military withdrew due to the weakening of the Soviet economy and discouragement over their inability to gain control of Afghanistan.

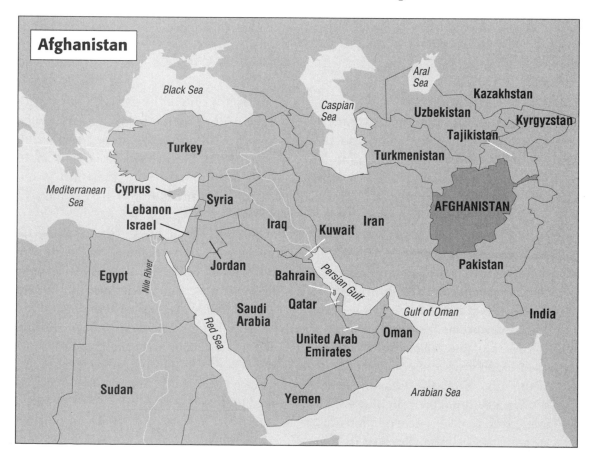

Afghanistan was free of the Soviets, but it had been hard hit by the years of fighting. The government had lost power. The economy was in ruins. Bombs had destroyed cities, roads, and other infrastructure. Many of the most intelligent and hardworking members of the population had moved to countries like the United States where they could live in peace. Journalist Rina Amiri gives further details: "For Afghans, the results of this war were devastating: 1.5 million dead, 5 million refugees, the exodus or death of its intellectual community, more than a million landmines, 500,000 widows, hundreds of thousands of orphans, and extremist Islamic groups in Afghanistan armed with some of the deadliest American weapons."[10]

The Enemy

Despite the plight of the Afghans, Americans heard little more about them until the mid-1990s, when the Pashtun-dominated Taliban (a group of fundamentalist Muslims) took over the country from warlords who had been engaged in a long-term power struggle after the Soviet withdrawal. Led by the mysterious and reclusive religious leader Mohammad Omar, called Mullah Omar, who came to power in 1996, the religious regime had set up a government and set about suppressing minority tribes and everyone else who disagreed with their conservative theology.

At the same time, the Taliban banned all Western customs from Afghan society and instituted sharia (Islamic religious law) throughout the country. News reports in-

formed Americans of the Taliban's harsh restrictions on the civilian population, particularly its oppression of women. They were forbidden to work or attend school and could not go out in public unless they were escorted and covered with a blanketlike *burka* that concealed even their eyes. Rules dictated men's appearance as well, and activities such as listening to music, using a computer, and even flying a kite were forbidden.

Reports also detailed public beatings and executions without the benefit of a trial. In accordance with sharia, those caught in marital infidelity were shot, beheaded, or stoned. Thieves had their hands amputated. These acts earned the Taliban government the condemnation of countries throughout the world. "Afghanistan is obviously one of the great horror stories of the world today. It is a vexing and tragic mosaic of suffering. And its seemingly endless civil war exacerbates [worsens] an already dire humanitarian situation,"[11] observed U.S. Ambassador to the UN Richard Holbrooke in April 2000.

A small band of Afghan rebels—the Northern Alliance—banded together in 1996 to fight the Taliban and establish a more moderate government. Because the Taliban had confiscated a great deal of abandoned Soviet and American weaponry, however, the Alliance was unable to make significant headway. "The amount of progress we have achieved this year is remarkable," declared head of the Alliance Ahmed Shad Massoud in mid-2001, putting the best spin possible on their efforts. "Last year the Taliban were

Harsh Punishment

The Taliban regime was harsh and inflexible, particularly when it came to those who broke the law. A description of some of the punishments that were inflicted is included in Michael Griffin's book, *Reaping the Whirlwind: The Taliban Movement in Afghanistan*.

Despite the emphasis placed by the Taliban on law and order, their judicial procedure was summary [rapid] and non-consultative. Courts, often supervised by illiterate *mullah*, might try a dozen cases in a day in sessions where no provision was made for legal council and where the presumption of innocence was absent. The gravest sentences, moreover, were carried out in public with a clear view to impressing spectators with the terror of the court. In February 1996 in Khost, two Afghans accused of murder were riddled with bullets in front of 20,000 people by the fathers of their victims in accordance with *qisas* [an-eye-for-an-eye justice]. In Herat, a young man was publicly hung from a crane, having confessed to killing two Taliban. Spectators said that he had been clearly beaten 'close to death' before arriving at the execution spot. In several of the 20 or so reported *hadud* [amputation] cases, hands or feet were summarily axed by Taliban guards without the benefit of a court appearance.

Cruel public executions were common punishment for Afghans who broke the law or opposed Taliban rule.

saying, 'we have conquered all of Afghanistan and resistance is in a tiny Tajik-dominated part of the country.' But now we see the revival of resistance all over Afghanistan." [12] Despite his brave words, Massoud was assassinated by al-Qaeda suicide bombers on September 9, 2001, leaving the Alliance even weaker than before.

The Terrorists

Although the Taliban was restrictive of its own people, it allowed members of al-Qaeda—Osama bin Laden's terrorist organization—to live and operate freely within the boundaries of the country. Americans did not take

serious note of bin Laden until August 1998, when, in response to attacks on U.S. embassies in Kenya and Tanzania, President Bill Clinton ordered the launch of cruise missiles at several al-Qaeda terrorist training camps in eastern Afghanistan.

Al-Qaeda had been formed in the 1980s as a support network for mujahideen warriors who were fighting the Soviets. It soon developed, however, into an international terror organization, made up of conservative Muslims—many of them from countries

Osama bin Laden expresses his fervent hatred of Westerners in a videotaped message.

other than Afghanistan—who opposed all who did not share their way of thinking. Some of these were individuals or small groups of bin Laden sympathizers who carried out random acts of terror on their own. Others were a close band of associates who helped bin Laden plan and carry out devastating attacks such as those on the World Trade Center and the Pentagon. These associates included his second-in-command, Egyptian-born Ayman al-Zawahiri; Abu Zubaydah, a Palestinian, who recruited future terrorists; and Mohammed Atef, also Egyptian, who would be indicted for the 1998 embassy bombings in Tanzania and Kenya. (Atef was killed in the war in Afghanistan in November 2001.)

Bin Laden himself, a friend of Mullah Omar, was a multimillionaire from Saudi Arabia. Dedicated, well-educated, and highly intelligent, he was also attractive—tall, handsome, and soft-spoken. His cultivated manner, however, hid his determination to eradicate everyone who disagreed with his conservative Muslim beliefs, including Jews, Christians, and such Muslim "heretics" as the Saudi Arabian government, who compromised with the West.

Bin Laden's hatred of the United States intensified after 1990, when Iraqi leader Saddam Hussein invaded the nation of Kuwait with the intent to occupy it and control its oil reserves. After the invasion, a coalition of nations led by the United States launched Operation Desert Storm, which lasted from January 15 to February 28, 1991. As part of its cooperative efforts during the war, the Saudi government gave American military forces permission to fight from bases in Arabia.

To bin Laden, this was the ultimate betrayal of Islam. From the standpoint of his radical theology, Christians were infidels and the eternal enemies of Muslims. Saudi Arabia was the birthplace of Islam, and he believed that Islamic holy places such as the Sacred Mosque in Mecca and the Prophet Muhammad's tomb in Medina were defiled simply by the American presence in his country. He vowed never to rest until all Westerners were expelled from Arabia and the Middle East.

Call to War

In 1996, bin Laden issued a worldwide fatwa (Islamic religious edict) declaring war against the United States and calling for the expulsion of U.S. military forces from the Middle East. In 1998, he broadened that declaration to call for the killing of all Americans and their allies throughout the world. He stated, "We . . . call on every Muslim who believes in God . . . to comply with God's order to kill the Americans. . . . We also call on Muslim Ulema [clerics], leaders, youths, and soldiers to launch the raid on Satan's US troops and the devil's supporters . . . that they may learn a lesson." [13]

Not until October 2000 and the bombing of the USS *Cole*, however, did ordinary Americans realize that bin Laden was in deadly earnest in his war against their country. The bold attack on an American vessel and the deaths of so many young

Americans not only stirred up the country's indignation, it revealed that al-Qaeda could not be ignored. Arizona congressman Jim Kolbe noted shortly after the bombing:

> Those who carried out the attack possessed considerable physical courage, just as did the Kamikaze pilots who crashed their aircraft into American warships in 1945. Those who planned and organized the attack apparently exhibited skill in picking the target and getting into position to strike.
>
> These are clever, crafty opponents arraigned [standing] against us. To deal with the terrorist threat we have to use every capability at our disposal. It does not help our efforts in fighting these enemies to hold them in contempt or pretend that they are cowards.[14]

The General

By October 2001—three weeks after the September 11 attacks—the American military was well aware of the ruthlessness of bin Laden and al-Qaeda. Troops had been ordered to be on an immediate wartime footing so they could defend themselves and the United States if further attacks seemed imminent. Plans for retaliation against the enemy had been pulled together quickly. "Within an hour [of the September 11 attacks], we started our broad planning to respond in some way,"[15] stated Lieutenant General Charles Wald, a senior official who was at the Pentagon on September 11.

General Tommy Ray Franks helped create a strategic plan to oust the Taliban and defeat al-Qaeda.

General Tommy Ray Franks, a tough, no-nonsense veteran of both the Vietnam War and Operation Desert Storm, was the commander placed in charge of the future war in Afghanistan. Born in Oklahoma in

1947, Franks had grown up in Texas, had joined the army in 1963, and earned three Purple Hearts and three Bronze Stars for heroic service in Vietnam in 1967–1968. In Desert Storm, he oversaw tactical units battling from helicopters and on the ground.

Franks worked his way through the ranks of the military until President Bill Clinton appointed him head of Central Command (CENTCOM) in June 2000. CENTCOM was one of nine unified combatant commands that controlled U.S. combat forces around the world. The others were the European Command, Pacific Command, Joint Forces Command, Southern Command, Space Command, Special Operations Command, Transportation Command, and Strategic Command. All commands were made up of military forces from two or more services and were organized into regions or categories known as Areas of Responsibility (AOR).

As head of CENTCOM, Franks was responsible for all army, navy, air force, and marine units that operated in an AOR encompassing twenty-five nations. It stretched from northern Africa and the Persian Gulf to southwest Asia. Franks's forces totaled up to 25,000 men and women, between 175 and 200 aircraft, and 30 naval vessels.

The general was in Crete en route to Pakistan when the September 11, 2001, attacks occurred. As he watched news footage showing the second airliner crashing into the World Trade Center tower, he guessed the implications of the event. "There was no doubt in my mind that this was a terrorist act," he stated. "I guess my sense was that Central Command would be very much involved in what would happen post 9/11 simply because, of the 25 countries in our area of responsibility, there are a number of sponsors of state terrorism." [16]

Franks was right—the military's primary task was soon defined. He was directed to remove the repressive Taliban regime that ruled Afghanistan and condoned terrorism ·against the West. He was also told to hunt down Osama bin Laden and other key

Know Your Enemy

In seeking to interview General Tommy Franks after September 11, 2001, news reporters learned that he was a very private man who gave few interviews. Cal Fussman of *Esquire* magazine was able to talk to the general, however, and asked him how he hoped to defeat Osama bin Laden. Franks's reply is included in Fussman's article, "What I've Learned," and can be accessed on the Internet at www.esquire.com.

It's helpful to understand what motivates Osama bin Laden, to understand what he treasures. Because human beings will generally respond to stimuli of things that are important to them. Knowing him as a thinker is not as important to me as knowing what's precious to him. His family is important to him. His ability to wield power is important to him. His ability to communicate. His ability to move money. We will work every thread of his existence until the work is done. Over time, we surely will either capture him or kill him.

members of his al-Qaeda network. The task promised to be long and arduous, but Franks was extremely confident that his men and women were up to the challenge. "There is no doubt that America will solve this problem of global terrorism," he emphasized. "It's only a matter of time, and I think this country has infinite patience."[17]

The Plan

Working with other military leaders as well as President George W. Bush and Secretary of Defense Donald Rumsfeld, Franks created a plan that he believed would defeat the enemy in Afghanistan in the shortest period of time. It would not involve fighting the Afghan people, but rather Taliban and al-Qaeda forces living in Afghanistan. It would achieve its goals through military might, high-tech capabilities, and by assisting the Northern Alliance and other rebel Afghans in their efforts to topple the Taliban government.

Franks decided that the best approach would be to begin with precision air attacks, using the latest high-tech weaponry such as unmanned surveillance planes and "smart bombs." These could knock out pockets of the enemy while lessening the risk of harming innocent civilians. Combined with that would be the utilization of elite U.S. forces such as the Green Berets, Army Rangers, and Delta Forces who could be dropped into the country under cover of darkness. These troops were highly trained to operate in the toughest and most sensitive wartime situations. They were also capable of carrying out missions without close supervision from superiors.

"The Partnership of Nations Is Here to Help"

Another flyer in the series, "The Partnership of Nations Is Here to Help," which was dropped over Afghanistan shortly after the war began in October 2001, assured the Afghan people that the United States had no intention of harming them. The text of other flyers in the series can be accessed on the Internet at www.cnn.com.

We are here to take measures against the terrorists that have rooted themselves in your country. It is not you, the honorable people of Afghanistan, who are targeted, but those who would oppress you, seek to bend you to their own will, and make you their slaves. . . .

We have no wish to hurt you, the innocent people of Afghanistan. Stay away from military installations, government buildings, terrorist camps, roads, factories, or bridges. If you are near these places, then you must move away from them. Seek a safe place, and stay well away from anything that might be a target. We do not wish to harm you.

With your help, this conflict can be over soon. And once again, Afghanistan will belong to you, and not to tyrants or outsiders. Then, you will reclaim your place among the nations of the world, and return to the honored place your country once held. Remember, we are here to help you to be free from this terrorism, despotism, and the fear and pain they bring with them. This is the best way to restore honor and dignity and make your country a free nation again.

Ground crew technicians transport a load of laser-guided bombs that will be used for air strikes on Afghanistan.

At the same time that Franks was forming plans for his own military, President Bush pulled together an international coalition of countries willing to support the war effort. These ranged from staunch allies such as Great Britain to former enemies such as Russia. All promised to help in ways that they judged appropriate. Some, such as Britain and Australia, provided troops. Some, such as Belgium, provided humanitarian aid and support to civilians. Some promised money, while others allowed U.S. military planes to use their airspace—fly over their countries—in order to reach Afghanistan. Deputy Secretary of State Richard Armitage noted, "We've got many countries who have actively sought us in or-der to engage in military activities with us. We've got overflight rights from over 26 countries, and we've got basing agreements with about 21 countries right now."[18]

"Ready to Get in the Game"

When launched, Franks's plans translated into a rush of activity on military bases across the country. Troop and equipment transport planes were moved to locales where they could pick up men and women and carry them overseas. Aircraft carriers, fighter jets, B-52 bombers, and flying tanker planes were dispatched to the Persian Gulf and the region around Afghanistan to be part of the first phase of the fighting. Special-operations forces were called back to duty at Fort Bragg, North Carolina; Fort Lewis, Washington; Fort Campbell, Kentucky; and Fort Carson, Colorado, and stood by, ready to be shipped out.

Military reservists and other support personnel were told to be ready in case they were needed in the near future. "This is the opening kickoff and we're ready to get in the game," said Colonel Kip Self of the Air Mobility Command at McGuire Air Force Base in New Jersey. His command was responsible for helping to move troops and equipment into a war theater. "Mo-bility is what we do here and our job is to get out of here and set up operations as rapidly as possible. We're almost like a big corporation moving. Our job is to take what is done here at McGuire and perform it overseas."[19]

As the days passed, the reality of the on-coming war dawned on the country, the troops, and the families they would leave behind. Fear, concern, and anticipation mixed uncomfortably with the pain that had been inflicted on September 11. "It's like a nightmare," said one mother as she waited to see if her son's unit would be shipped overseas. "You want to say it's not really true. It's not really happening. But it is happening. It's happening."[20]

Chapter 2

Getting Ready to Go

For U.S. troops, the call to war was validation for months or years of training and an opportunity to take their place among the ranks of so many other military personnel who had served and sacrificed for their country. Getting ready to go, however, was a stressful time, full of hectic preparation and emotional ups and downs for everyone from enlistees to high-ranking officers. All were optimistic, but no one knew what the future would hold. "You never know how you're going to do and how you're going to respond," said Colonel Arnold Bray, commander of the Eighty-second Airborne Division stationed in Fort Bragg, North Carolina. "[But] training is what you fall back on. Everyone here is well trained. What that means in real life, we're about to find out."[21]

Volunteer Armed Services

Those who prepared to go to Afghanistan in 2001 were much like the forces who fought in previous conflicts such as World War II and the Vietnam War. They were intelligent, well trained, adaptable, and equipped with the best weapons and gear. The majority were young, physically fit males from lower-middle-class families. All loved their country and the freedom and opportunity it offered. Most had never served in a previous war but were prepared to step forth and do their part.

Despite the similarities to troops of earlier generations, there were some significant differences as well. In earlier wars, the U.S. Selective Service System was responsible for drafting eligible young men to maintain adequate numbers in the military. Some 10 million were drafted during World War II, 1.5 million during the Korean War, and 1.7 million during the Vietnam War. Not all who were drafted were enthusiastic about the service, especially during Vietnam, and thus some often gave less than 100 percent commitment when it came to their work.

The draft ended in July 1973, and the modern military became entirely reliant on volunteers at that time. New members chose to join, often as a result of recruiting. Recruiters regularly visited high schools to promote the U.S. Army, Navy, Air Force, and Marines as viable postgraduate options. Professionalism, quality of life, good pay, and the promise of upward mobility were emphasized. Well-done television advertisements and catchy slogans such as "Be All That You Can Be" and "Be an Army of One" also aimed to motivate a young audience.

The efforts were successful. Thousands of serious, energetic young men opted to use the military as a launching pad for their careers. Many were minorities who realized that in the service they had a better chance to be judged on performance and merit rather than race. In 1972, about 17 percent of the army was African American, but by 1996, African Americans made up more than 30 percent of the army and almost 22 percent of the total enlisted forces.

Young women also began enlisting in greater numbers. In 1972, slightly more than 2 percent of the army was female. In 2000, women composed about 15 percent of the army, 13 percent of the navy, 19 percent of the air force, and 6 percent of the marines. No women in the military were allowed to participate in certain areas or situations such as Special Forces or submarines, but in all other areas—even combat—they found opportunities to serve. Positions ranged from supply clerks to ship commanders. "There have been ups and downs," says Carolyn Becraft, deputy assistant secretary of defense

Room for Women

As more women joined the military, they were given opportunities to pursue careers as diverse as shop managers and pharmacists. One meteorologist explains how her work plays an unexpectedly important role in war. Her sketch, and those of other military women, is included on the Internet at www.militarywoman.org.

In the army we do meteorology, but it's not the conventional thinking of what a meteorologist does. We do take weather reports like wind direction, humidity, temperature, and so on, but what we do not do is to make forecasts. No, we don't predict the weather. The air force and the navy do that, although we do help them. . . .

So maybe you're thinking, why exactly does the field artillery need us? Because, if you're into weapons or hunt and such, then you probably know that temperature and wind direction affect a projectile as it's moving through the air. Making sense now? And when you're talking about things like missiles and huge projectiles that go higher and farther than bullet rounds, you need to know the atmospheric conditions. The atmosphere changes the higher you go, and it can throw a round off target from 50 to 100 meters over or under. Also, if a nuclear missile is used, the wind blows the radiation for miles, [so] we also give the wind direction so the FDC [fire direction control, which computes the effects of weather on the trajectory of shells and missiles] can put that information out to the surrounding support.

Rifle training is just one of the skills that prepares enlistees in the military for active duty.

under President Bill Clinton. "But they [women] now are a larger percentage of the military, and they have higher ranks, and, by all accounts, they're performing very well."[22]

The Enlistees

The events of September 11 and the weeks following sparked increased interest in military service from civilians from all walks of life. Those persons who had served in active duty before were often inclined to offer their services again. Young people who had given little thought to military service in the past were attracted as well. "After September 11, my perspective on life changed," said Amy Ting, who had previously given up medical studies to study acting in New York City. "I have always wanted to help people, so I de-

cided to go back to pursuing the medical field. . . . [And] the more I learned about the Air Force, the more I wanted to be a part of it."[23] Ting joined the Air Force and began training to become a physical therapist.

While patriotism was an underlying factor in many enlistees' decision making, there were those who joined for practical reasons as well. Some wanted to get away from home, to "see the world," and to be on their own as adults. Some joined because they could also qualify for education benefit programs (G.I. Bills) that would later pay for college. Some joined to challenge themselves both physically and mentally. "I grew up on the west side of Chicago—a bad neighborhood with drug dealers and crime," said Richard Jones. "This is something I want to do to see if I can do it.... By starting something new I'm showing my brothers that they can do it, too. They're like my number one priority, my brothers and my mother."[24]

No matter what their motivation, all enlistees found that their resolve was tested when they faced nine weeks of demanding basic training and then two months to a year of specialization before they could be a part of any military campaign. Basic training, designed to instruct and prepare recruits for life as soldiers, was an ordeal even for the best. Between the first week—when all were given vaccines, physical assessment tests, and classroom instruction—and the ninth, when they graduated, recruits were confronted with a variety of learning situations. All had to master skills such as first aid, map and compass reading, and drill (marching). All went through constant fitness training while practicing unarmed combat; marksmanship; throwing hand grenades; and dealing with nuclear, biological, and chemical threats. Many times the instruction was unpleasant, but most enlistees grew stronger and more confident because of it. "Coming into basic training, I really wasn't all that excited about working with the M16 rifle," observed Michelle Boatner, a new recruit at Fort Jackson, South Carolina. "But now the more I handle it, I'm becoming more comfortable with it. There's just a sense of power that

you get when you have this weapon in your hand."[25]

The final week of basic training wrapped up with a seventy-two-hour challenge that tested everything the enlistees had learned. Successful completion marked the passage from civilians to soldiers, sailors, airmen, and marines. "Soldiers . . . feel like they are pushed both physically and mentally, and they are proud of what they have done,"[26] stated Army Major General John A. Van Alstyne, commander of Fort Jackson, South Carolina.

With the completion of basic training, soldiers then went on to a military occupational specialty (MOS). This could include health care specialist, satellite-systems communications operator, construction engineering supervisor, and a host of other specialities. Training was specific for each. Combat engineers, for instance, were given six weeks of advanced and hands-on training in such subjects as basic engineering principles, road maintenance and repair, bridge building, and use of hand and power tools. Their responsibilities would eventually include placing and detonating explosives, directing the construction of fighting positions, and conducting reconnaissance operations.

Infantrymen, on the other hand, required five weeks of formal training in squad maneuvers, target practice, and war games in the field, with ongoing training continuing thereafter to keep them in a constant state of readiness. "There is much more to being an infantryman than being technically and tactically competent. This is a business of leading and knowing men; a line of work that potentially puts you in a position to cause men to die,"[27] says infantryman Patrick D. McGowen, who served for twenty years.

Special Forces

Some of the most challenging of all MOSs were those for special operations forces. These included Army Special Forces (Green Berets), Rangers (who specialized as strike forces), and Delta Forces (who specialized

in hostage release); navy SEALs; Marine Force Recon; and Air Force Special Ops. In Afghanistan, for the first time in any war, special-operations forces were going to carry out most of the combat, so their presence and expertise would be even more vital than in earlier conflicts.

Special operations forces were physically tough, skilled in unconventional warfare, and ready at a moment's notice to be

Army Rangers train in hostile environments to be ready for any mission.

Operational Detachment Alpha

Special Forces—also known as Green Berets—made up the majority of troops on the ground during the early months of the war. The men were trained to be self-sufficient, able to cope with the toughest of situations. A description of some of their responsibilities is included below, and more information can be found on the Internet at http://sf.goarmy.com.

Special Forces groups are organized in small teams of 12 men—aka [also known as] Operational Detachment Alpha (ODA). Each soldier in an ODA is specially trained and crossed trained in different disciplines. . . .

A captain [is] responsible for mission organization, outfitting his team, and the debriefing [explanation] of mission objectives. . . . Special Forces Weapons Sergeants are . . . capable of maintaining and operating a wide variety of U.S., Allied, and other foreign weaponry. . . . Some of [Special Forces Engineering Sergeants'] tasks may include working in demolitions, explosives, land and water navigation duties . . . , reconnaissance and sabotage operations.

Special Forces Medical Sergeants are considered to be some of the finest first-response/trauma medical technicians in the world. Though they're primarily trained with an emphasis on trauma, they also have a working knowledge of dentistry, veterinary care, public sanitation . . . and optometry. . . .

Special Forces Communication Sergeants operate every kind of communications gear from encrypted satellite communication systems to old-style high-frequency Morse Code systems. Since many SF [Special Forces] missions require being behind the lines in hostile areas, each team is given an 18F intelligence specialist. The 18F collects and evaluates information for transmission, and supplies vital data on the enemy.

sent on missions anywhere in the world. Not only had they been through basic training, they also learned infantry and airborne (paratrooper) skills, and had taken a variety of leadership, physical training, and survival courses. "I've trained in desert, urban, jungle, and alpine,"[28] noted Special Forces weapons sergeant Loren Schaffer. After passing these challenges, all went on to other qualification courses where they received training in such subjects as land navigation, survival, evasion, resistance, and escape. Some also received "live environment training" where they prepared to become a virtual citizen of another country by immersing themselves in the language, culture, and traditions of the specific society.

Total training time for these forces sometimes lasted up to four years, but Secretary of Defense Donald Rumsfeld and other military leaders were convinced that the extra time and training were an important factor in allowing the U.S. military to be successful in war, especially a war against terrorism. "The global nature of the war, the nature of the enemy and the need for fast, efficient operations in hunting down and rooting out terrorist networks around the world have all contributed to the need for an expanded role for the special operations forces,"[29] Rumsfeld said in January 2003.

The Reservists

Active recruiting successfully drew thousands of young, highly motivated volunteers into the military but, despite a steady stream of enlistees, the numbers did not make up a force as large as that sustained during the years of the draft. At the peak of the Vietnam War in 1968, enrollment topped 3 million; in 1990, it was about 2 million. The smaller fighting force was adequate for peacetime, but when Operation Desert Storm commenced in 1991, a larger military was needed. Thus, the military turned to National Guard and reserve forces to fight in the war. These reservists were those who were trained in a military specialty, but worked at jobs in the private sector unless they were needed. For instance, air force pilot Westel W. Willoughby was a farmer. Army surgeon William C. Devries had his own private practice. Army pharmacy technician Tobie Wethington was a computer technician with AmericaOnline.

During the Vietnam War, the military called up only 3,000 reservists. In Desert Storm, 135,000 reservists were called. "We were there and we were essential," said Lieutenant General Thomas J. Plewes. "We established a new basis for where we moved in the future."[30]

For the war in Afghanistan, more than fifty thousand reservists were needed to help boost the numbers in the military. Most were pleased to be called. "This country means the world to me," stated one air force colonel who was an American Airlines pilot in civilian life. "I am thrilled and honored to do my part in this war."[31]

Nevertheless, deployment often meant serious, unexpected disruption of their normal lives. Husbands or wives who were left behind became single parents, taking on unfamiliar family responsibilities alone. Teachers had to leave their classrooms, nurses their patients, and construction workers their projects.

Brian Perry put his law practice aside when he was assigned to the Army Joint Inter-Agency Task Force, a team that helped coordinate coalition actions in Afghanistan. Despite the inconvenience, he went willingly and approved of the use of reservists in the war. "The General had come up with the idea to assign senior, staff officers [reservists] to the task force. . . . They, like me, would . . . bring civilian-acquired skills to the war. Active-duty soldiers are single-faceted. Reservists are multi-functional."[32]

Reservists were not the only ones to cope with disrupted schedules. Their employers were often asked to grant leaves at a moment's notice. Despite the complications, most reservists had no trouble getting time away, especially after September 11. "This time around, we have many more employers, both public and private, who are matching the salaries—or continuing the salaries if a military salary is significantly less—of their employees,"[33] explained Plewes. Reservists who worked for a company were also guaranteed that they would find their old jobs waiting for them when they finished their terms of service.

Despite the fact that they were service members, the call alerting reservists to report for duty took many by surprise. "People . . . go into the Guard or Reserve and get the educational benefits, stuff like that, but they never believe anything will happen," explained reservist Charles Warren, who also served in the air force in Operation Desert Storm. "When they do get the call up [they say], 'I didn't sign up for this.' Well, yes, you did." [34]

Even those who expected the call found it unsettling. "I'm a little bit apprehensive, not knowing what you're going to face or who you're going to face," explains Israel "Ray" Rios, a municipal courts supervisor and army reservist. "You can say you're ready, but mentally you might be hesitant, not knowing what kind of forces you're going to be facing." [35]

Painful Partings

As plans for war took shape, troops and reservists across the United States waited to see the role they would play in the upcoming conflict. For those in specialized units such as the "Screaming Eagles" (101st Army Airborne Division) at Fort Campbell, Kentucky, the call to fight was inevitable. The legendary air assault unit had been the first American unit to set foot in Nazi-occupied France during World War II. It had taken part in the ill-fated Tet Offensive in Vietnam, and had been involved in the opening engagements of Operation Desert Storm. It always had its gear packed in order to be able to leave within thirty-six hours. "It's clear to me and the troops that something big is going to happen," stated the fort's commander, General Richard A. Cody. "A lot of people will be involved. The Army will be involved. This division will be involved." [36]

Although no one was given specific information about their ultimate duties or where they would be posted, all troops were told to report to a base or meeting place at

Call to Action

Cheryl Knight, director of clinical services for pediatric oncology at Children's Hospital in Orange County, California, is also a military reservist, trained to be a flight nurse in case of war. The account of her call to service, titled "Knight's Tale: A Call to Action for Nurse Reservist," can be read in its entirety at www.nurseweek.com on the Internet.

"Our unit was put on stand by the night of September 11. I had to report to March Air Force Base near San Bernardino, where I spent the next six days waiting to be sent to New York City." Knight's unit never did fly to the East Coast, but the experience was memorable nonetheless.

"It was my first time being called up in seven years in the Air Force Reserve," said Knight, who has been a nurse for 21 years. Even though she didn't leave her home state, she said the call up affected her significantly. "Being activated had a big impact on my family and me. It's scary. It's hard for the families when you're activated." Knight's husband and children, the youngest of whom is 10, didn't know when she left when they would see her again.

A soldier bids a tender farewell to his wife before departing for Afghanistan.

a specific time. Notification was commonly by telephone or letter and often allowed those involved only a few days to set their lives in order before they departed.

The first step involved practicalities such as making or updating wills. Insurance coverage had to be checked. Arrangements were made for bills to be paid and for paychecks to be properly routed and processed. Employers were notified. "It didn't cause much trouble in my unit [at the hospital]," explained Cheryl Knight who nurses at Children's Hospital of Orange County, Califor-

nia. "There are others ready to take on my work. Being called up isn't going to impact the hospital much."[37]

The next step was more difficult—taking leave of family and friends. Those who were going to fight the war were generally motivated and upbeat, and for some military wives and husbands, the parting was a normal part of life. They had grown used to the fact that they would be left to raise children and make decisions on their own. Still, all knew that they would miss their spouses, just as they would miss having someone to share decision making with. "When I need his insight, I have to make that decision [on my own]. I wonder if something goes wrong because of my decision, could I live with that?"[38] said Kim Newland, who was raising three teenage daughters.

Most of those who were left behind were naturally fearful that they would never see their loved one again, however. Tears were common during the waiting period and upon parting. Children, too, were teary eyed and often confused because they did not know where a parent was going or when he or she would be back. "It's always hard for a family to get used to,"[39] says reservist Michelle Cianci. And Israel Rios voiced the thoughts that were in the back of everyone's mind, "My wife's been telling me if you have to go, do your duty the best way you can. Hopefully, you'll come back walking instead of in a coffin."[40]

"Fall Out and Get Hitched"

Many single men and women who received word that they were going off to war decided that the time was right to finalize commitments they had made to significant others. New engagements were common. So were weddings, with at least one magistrate at Fort Bragg, North Carolina, performing twelve ceremonies a day instead of the usual two or three.

Plans for traditional ceremonies were often modified to simpler services. Kristy Steele and her husband got married September 18, 2001, on the spur of the moment in hiking boots and rubber beach sandals. Corey Gilliland got married in his battle dress uniform because his more formal clothes were packed. "We've got whole companies coming in together," joked sheriff's deputy Robbie Johnson, a justice of the peace in Fayetteville, North Carolina. "It's, 'Fall out and get hitched.'"[41]

The actual departure often eased the pain for troops who had war preparations to distract their thoughts. Those who waited at home, however, tried to cope in different ways. A few followed the war in detail, watching the evening news on the chance that they could catch a glimpse of a spouse, son, or daughter. Others avoided every report, a strategy that shielded them from rumors and inaccurate information that could be worrisome.

Many new wives chose to return to their parents' home where they could have family support. Others got involved with their work or took part in activities at school or church that made time pass more quickly. Support groups and friends in similar circumstances were helpful as well. Karin, the wife of a naval aviator, says, "I made sure to surround myself with other military wives who could understand what I was going through."[42]

Going to War

With the partings behind them, the troops faced transport to the war zone. If the trip was by air, it could take place relatively quickly. Journeys by ship took longer. The

USS *Carl Vinson* and its battle group of destroyers, guided-missile cruisers, a submarine, and other vessels, had been heading to an assignment in the Middle East when the September 11 attacks occurred, so it arrived in the Indian Ocean in just days. The USS *Bataan*, on the other hand, had set out from Norfolk, Virginia, on September 27, 2001, to carry out scheduled war exercises with Egypt in November. With members of the Twenty-sixth Marine Expeditionary Unit aboard, it finally arrived off the coast of Pakistan in mid-December. One member of the crew observed on December 19, "This past week, the majority of the Twenty-sixth Marine Expeditionary Unit completed its third leg of the 'tri-continental deployment.' The first stop was Europe at Rota, Spain; then came Africa with our exercises in Egypt; and now, with our members in Pakistan and Afghanistan, we hit Asia!"[43]

Huge aircraft carriers like the USS Kitty Hawk *serve as mobile bases of operation.*

The United States elected to utilize such aircraft carriers not only as transport and attack vessels, but also as bases of operations during the war. Afghanistan was surrounded by nations that did not welcome an American presence, so basing troops within their borders was not feasible. A few bases existed in the neighboring countries of Uzbekistan and Pakistan, but both countries preferred that troops stationed there be involved primarily with search, rescue, and humanitarian operations.

Floating in international waters in the Indian Ocean, however, carriers were beyond the jurisdiction of other countries. They were also relatively safe and secure stations for military aircraft as well as those who flew and serviced them. In a unique move, the military also elected to turn one carrier, the USS *Kitty Hawk,* into a floating operations base for special operations forces. The carrier, usually headquartered in Japan, left her strike jets behind and took on dozens of helicopters and special forces troops who took part in the earliest attacks on the Taliban. As one defense official who chose to remain anonymous observed, "The *Kitty Hawk* is a significant piece of sovereign US real estate in easy reach of key targets."[44]

Life on these carriers, which carried up to five thousand people, was similar to living on a military base. Each carrier had an airport, hospital, pharmacy, police department, jail, and fire department. Massive kitchens turned out meals three times a day. Sleeping quarters were barrackslike and sometimes crowded. On the USS *Carl Vinson,* six restaurants, two stores, a library, a gym, and a TV studio provided outlets for relaxation.

Those aboard filled their days with work that ranged from ministering to the religious and emotional needs of the crew to navigating the carrier to its destination. "Very rarely is it true that there's 'nothing to do' out here in the 'Med' [Mediterranean Sea] while on deployment," wrote one crewmember:

> There are any number of tasks that must be accomplished and some of them on a daily basis. For example, there's vehicle and equipment maintenance, inventorying and ordering of all supplies in each department or section, clean up and repair of spaces and even personal articles, and, of course, the ever necessary maintenance of physical readiness for any job, exercise, or mission that might have to be accomplished.[45]

No matter how long or how short the journey to their destination, all crewmembers spent the time mentally and physically preparing themselves for the task ahead. They worked out in the gym and sat through periods of instruction. They rehearsed what they would do when faced with an objective and practiced combat skills and survival techniques. "We are no longer in a time of training. We are in a time of preparation,"[46] said marine corporal Terrence C. York aboard the USS *Bataan* in November 2001.

In that time of preparation, the dangers and hardships they would face were still unknown. Those heading to Afghanistan, however, were well aware that they were the front line of a world force that could not allow terrorism to continue. President George W. Bush had made an effective point on November 11, 2002. "The evildoers struck, and when they did, they aroused a mighty land, a land of compassionate people, a land who wants to help a neighbor in need. . . . We sent a loud message to the world: We will not be cowed by a few. We sent another message to the world: Together we're going to bring these people to justice. And that's exactly what we're going to do." [47]

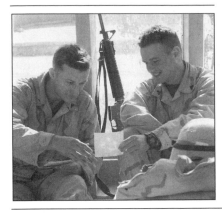

Chapter 3

Living in "the 'Stan"

The war in Afghanistan began as earlier wars had begun—with the establishment of troops and equipment near the region where the action would take place. Although all forces had received detailed information about the environment and living conditions with which they would be coping, none were entirely prepared for the austere and treacherous life they would lead in "the 'Stan," as they soon nicknamed the rugged country that lay half a globe away from the United States. Neverthless, with the support of their leaders, Americans at home, and each other, most survived and even enjoyed limited periods of fun during their time overseas.

Dangerous Country

Few American soldiers set foot in Afghanistan in the first weeks of the war, and those who did were elite special operations commandos who were inserted and then removed immediately after they accomplished a specific mission. Many of these missions lasted just hours and were not reported to the public or were explained in the most general of terms. "There are certain things taking place from the air and things from time to time being coordinated with the ground,"[48] stated Defense Secretary Donald Rumsfeld, emphasizing that operations were top secret to prevent the enemy from being forewarned.

Beginning in mid-October, however, as intense bombing of the Taliban by U.S. and British forces began, the United States began deploying Special Forces units into Afghanistan on longer missions designed to help support the Northern Alliance. One of the primary U.S. units was Operational Detachment Alpha 595, a twelve-man team assigned to assist Alliance leader Abdul Rashid Dostum. Dostum conducted guerrilla operations near the city of Mazār-e Sharīf with his militia, who numbered in the thousands. Detachment Alpha 595 was dropped into the country by helicopter to live and fight beside the Alliance.

Living conditions were strenuous and demanding for the unit. They had no formal base of operations and began their work in a remote valley in northern Afghanistan. Few people resided there. Travel was difficult in the steep, rocky terrain. In the daytime, temperatures could rise to above one hundred degrees. At night, they dipped below freezing.

One of the most constant elements in their environment was dust. Years of drought had left much of the country covered with a fine, dry powder that blew freely in the strong winds that were common in the region. Dust covered trees, buildings, and human beings. It filled the sky with an orangish tan haze and turned the world light brown. Dust filtered into weapons and communications gear and made constant cleaning of equipment necessary to avoid malfunctions. Soldiers were forced to cover their faces with goggles and scarves in order to see and breathe.

While dust and dirt were irritants, thousands of unexploded land mines that littered the country were real and constant dangers. During past wars, Soviet, Afghan, and Taliban forces had planted the exploding ordnance thickly to deny territory to the enemy. Some were antipersonnel mines such as "Bouncing Bettys" that sprang up and exploded after being stepped on. Some were larger antitank mines. There were also thousands of unexploded cluster bombs, yellow tubes equipped with small wings that had been dropped from planes and lay scattered about. These were often picked up by chil-

U.S. Special Forces helped Northern Alliance leader Abdul Rashid Dostum fight the Taliban.

dren who thought they were toys. In fact, soldiers could see the effect of the explosives' devastating presence throughout the country. "Everywhere you go, there are people missing hands, arms, those with no legs. There are thousands and thousands of people throughout Afghanistan without limbs because of land mines,"[49] said Abdul Adil, an Afghan who worked on demining efforts in the country.

"Definitely Interesting"

The harsh environment and dangerous terrain of Afghanistan were only two of the challenges facing Alpha 595. Foremost was the test of their courage as they came face to face with their new allies. "We all had very heavy packs on our backs, just around a hundred pounds worth of equipment. . . . We came out the back of the helicopter through the dust and clouds. You saw the Afghans coming out to lead us. It was a tense time, and very eerie, because they wear robes with A-47s [automatic weapons] coming out of them,"[50] said one member of the unit. Another added, "It was like the sand people from 'Star Wars,' coming at you."[51]

Once they had determined that they were among friends, the Americans set about fitting in to their new surroundings. Far from cities and villages, they camped out with the rebels and were glad for rare opportunities when they had a roof over their heads. "We were sleeping in a cleaned out cattle stable," noted another member of the unit, remembering their first night in the country. "They had laid some carpets down on the ground. We had two or three pet mice and rats that were running around the area. That was our home for the next several days."[52]

In the desert or the nearby hills, they ate, slept, and kept warm by campfires and by the clothes they wore. Unlike more traditional units who dressed in uniforms and

helmets, they commonly favored an informal mix of camouflage, blue jeans, vests, and baseball hats. Because shaving was impossible under the circumstances, most let their beards grow, and some even donned native clothing in order to blend in with the Afghans.

Food was typical army supplies, commonly called "Meals Ready to Eat" (MREs). These were packages that served one person and included an entrée—meat loaf with gravy, Thai chicken, or chicken tetrazzini, among others—plus a side dish, dessert, and beverage. Despite the exotic names, most were mediocre when it came to taste and all had to be eaten with a spoon, which came in the package. Many American personnel grumbled when forced to eat MREs for too long, but Afghans saw them in a different light. "The troops that we were there with, they were starving," explained one team member. "So we began to share what little food we had with them. And this went a long ways towards establishing rapport [a good relationship]."[53]

Training had prepared special operations teams for rough conditions, poor food, and other hardships, but they were unprepared to use transportation favored by the Northern Alliance. The rebels traveled on horseback, using smaller native Afghan horses. The Americans were expected to do the same, despite the fact that some of them had never ridden a horse before. All gamely took the challenge, coping with primitive wooden saddles, the aggressive nature of the animals that had a tendency to fight, and

MREs

Meals Ready to Eat—brown plastic pouches that contain enough food for one meal—are standard military fare for soldiers in combat. They spark many complaints, but the food inside is much better than rations given to soldiers in earlier wars. Martin Savidge, one of the few journalists allowed in the war zone, gives his impression of MREs in an article titled "'Camp Candy Bar' and Thought for Food," found on the Internet at www.cnn.com.

The neat thing is that along with the entrée comes a heating pouch—no fires to give you away to the enemy. You slide the entrée pouch into a high-tech plastic sleeve and then add about an ounce of water [not included]. The resulting chemical reaction makes the meal steaming hot. . . .

There's usually a side dish, sometimes rice. Bread that's more of a biscuit than a slice. And a dessert such as pound cake, fudge brownie, fruit. There are also the condiments: salt, sugar, coffee, a powdered fruit drink and candy. . . . Lastly there's Tabasco sauce. The soldiers put it on, or in, everything. . . .

Many soldiers pass along recipes that would make Martha Stewart proud. For instance, mix the peaches, warmed, with a crumbled granola bar and—voila!—peach cobbler. There's also a recipe for 'Ranger Pudding' involving hot cocoa powder mixed into a paste with a dash of dry coffee creamer added. They say it's great with Tabasco.

A soldier tears open his ready-to-eat dinner packet. MREs provide hot and nutritious food, but they are often bland.

narrow mountain trails that had to be traveled at night. Covering more than eighteen miles of rough terrain in utter darkness was an unforgettable experience for some. One remembered, "While we were first riding . . . , you're looking around thinking, 'Here I am riding a horse in the middle of Afghanistan.' It's a little weird. It's kind of a little bit further out than the things you might have thought you'd normally be doing. It was definitely interesting, though."[54]

Camp Rhino

While Special Forces teams worked with the Northern Alliance, the United States began sending other troops to Afghanistan to establish bases and a more formal presence on the ground. On November 21, 2001, members of a navy SEAL team were dropped into southern Afghanistan by U.S. Special-Operations aircraft to check out the safety and usefulness of a small, abandoned airstrip prior to the marines landing there. The strip—nothing more than a bomb-pocked runway and a few deserted hangars—had been created and used by a wealthy Arab for hunting expeditions.

The SEALs marked the airfield and provided security when the first crew of five hundred marines landed on November 25, 2001. Six Chinook helicopters deposited the newcomers in the dead of night near the airstrip, which was located south of the city of Kandahar. Prepared for an enemy assault, the marines quickly reinforced security in the immediate area and then raised an American flag on a makeshift pole. "Marines take pride in raising the flag, and pride doesn't begin to describe our feelings today," said one platoon sergeant, "I hope these colors can be seen all the way across Afghanistan."[55]

Pass the Ammunition

Even on bases at Bagram and Kandahar, soldiers were on guard every moment against enemy attack. The constant presence of their firearms testified to that fact. Journalist Martin Savidge reported on the weapons requirement at the Kandahar base in "A Man of No Caliber," found on the Internet at www.cnn.com.

> Everybody here has a gun but me. . . . Military personnel must have their guns with them at all times. Everywhere. The shower line for instance. As I clutch my bar of soap and shampoo, the soldiers in front of me sport new M-4s [short barreled rifles]. . . . Guns are at the latrines, at chow, in the PX, at prayer. Sunday services rarely see a congregation so heavily armed. Amen and pass the ammunition.
>
> In the morning, joggers flit by in their shorts and T-shirts, looking like their urban counterparts back home. But those aren't Walkmans they hold in their hands. They're most likely M-9s, the Beretta pistol. . . . This is the ultimate example of a soldier being able to return fire while on the run. . . .
>
> Guns are everywhere here. From the front lines around the base to the line to call home. Face it, it's hard to have a war these days without them.

The new base was named Camp Rhino. The men stationed there knew that, in addition to fending off any enemy attacks, their first task was to survive the sand, howling winds, and freezing temperatures. Like the Special Forces teams before them, they were struck by the ruggedness of the land. "The main challenge in this country is dealing with the environment. There are huge dust storms here—so strong that sometimes you have problems breathing and seeing. As you can imagine, it really wreaks havoc with the helicopters,"[56] said army sergeant George Hildebrandt.

Using their ingenuity, the men first used cardboard packing material to erect walls around the combat operations center where delicate computers and other instruments were housed. Next, they dug foxholes in which they huddled until better accommodations could be established. Within days, hangars were cleared of bombs and booby traps, and many of the men took shelter inside, also using the buildings to protect their equipment. Despite the better protection and the most up-to-date cold and wind resistant uniforms and protective gear, all suffered from the elements.

Living conditions remained primitive at Camp Rhino. Toilets were simple pits in the ground. Campfires provided meager warmth. MREs were the only food available. Water was limited. Marine staff sergeant Eddie Barringer noted, "We were allotted four one-liter bottles of water a day. We would drink two and save two. That way, after a few days, you would have enough to wash your body."[57]

The Base at Kandahar

As the weeks passed, greater numbers of military forces moved into Afghanistan, and bases were established at Khowst, Mazār-e Sharīf, Kandahar International Airport, and Bagram Air Base. The majority of U.S. troops were stationed at the latter two.

For a time, there were few luxuries to be enjoyed even on larger bases. In December 2001, when marines captured the Kandahar airport from the Taliban, the facility was little more than a tiny cluster of bombed-out buildings with no water, electricity, or plumbing facilities. An abundance of rusting Soviet airplanes, helicopters, cars, and munitions cluttered the fields nearby.

As marines took over, they made do with quickly constructed facilities. A barbed wire fence was built around the airport, supported by posts made of large metal bomb containers, leftovers from the Soviets. Watchtowers were made of mobile stairways and old utility wagons. Bunkers were foxholes covered with corrugated steel and draped with old Soviet tents to hold in warmth. "Walking around, there are a lot of abandoned old cars," said Corporal Brent D. Rogers, a steelworker. "They come in handy. You can cut off pieces of a car and pretty much make anything."[58]

Despite marine ingenuity, living conditions were tough. Bathroom facilities were pit toilets surrounded by sheet metal

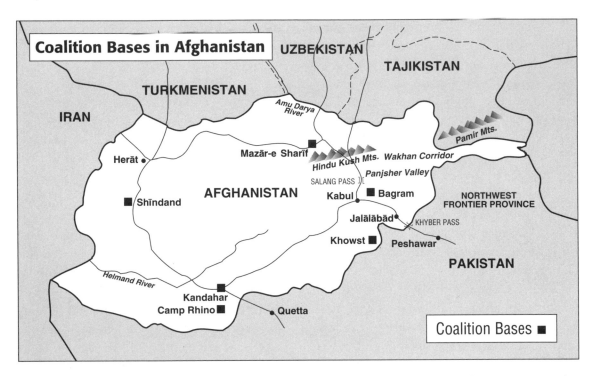

shelters. Waste was burned in metal drums, creating a nauseating stench. Soldiers bathed using baby wipes and shaved at hygiene stations where water was heated in metal buckets over propane heaters. At night, they slept shoulder to shoulder in tents, even when temperatures dipped below freezing. "You are in a place with 20 guys. There are no walls and no privacy. [And during the day], it's hot, anywhere from 95 to 112 degrees, no shade. You're wearing 40 pounds of gear. You have the fear of being shot or killed. . . . You could hear shots or explosions at night."[59] said engineer Michael Villacres.

The Base at Bagram

In December 2001, when troops first landed at Bagram Air Base, in the central part of Afghanistan, conditions there were as grim as at Kandahar. Signs in Russian were a reminder that the Soviets had used the base to launch aerial bombardments on the Afghans during the 1980s war. Discarded Soviet machinery had to be dragged out of abandoned hangars and other buildings before machine shops could be established. Thousands of unexploded land mines and bombs lay buried in the sand around the base, making it dangerous to step off cleared pavement.

As at Kandahar, soldiers at first ate MREs and made do with primitive, overcrowded toilet facilities and few showers. The Afghan dust was everywhere. "I just wish I could keep my hands clean for 10 minutes," said senior airman Josh Keener, "you feel dirty all the time."[60]

Danger from the enemy was very real at both bases. The perimeters repeatedly came under attack, usually at night, from rocket and small-arms fire. Soldiers were on the alert at all times and made sure that their counterstrikes were prompt and impressive. Operations officer captain Dan Greenwood directed a marine response to one enemy strike at Kandahar in early January 2002. The counterattack included M-16 assault rifles, grenade launchers, and cannons. "We used all the assets we have," he stated. "[Their assault] was a probe, based on three fronts. They were testing our defenses, and they'll think twice about hitting us again."[61]

Better Times

In late January 2002, marines at Kandahar transferred back to U.S. Navy ships in the Arabian Sea, while eight hundred members of the Army's 101st Airborne took their place on the base. At that time, military engineers began to make improvements there, constructing a chapel, laundry facilities, a mess hall, and foundations for tents.

Improvements were slowly made at Bagram as well. Because of its isolated setting, everything had to be shipped in by air. An Army and Air Force Exchange representative arrived twice a month to stock the small base store with fast-selling items like cookies, sodas, and chips. Even the nearest laundry was in Uzbekistan, and clothing was flown in and out of the base three times a week. "Your laundry comes back looking like chewing tobacco. Sometimes you get your laundry back. And sometimes you get somebody else's drawers [briefs],"[62] observed one soldier.

A marine shaves using rationed water at the hygiene station on the Kandahar base.

Eventually, both bases grew to the size of small cities and featured a multitude of facilities including a PX (post exchange, or base store), dining hall, post office, gas station, water treatment plant, and medical clinic complete with surgeons, dentists, and optometrists. Air conditioners cooled the barracks. Troops had access to computers, barbers and hairstylists, and barbecue grills. They were able to work out in gyms and call home from the communications tent. They could also buy magazines and electronic games in the PX.

Mama's Home Cooking

Food provisions improved with time as well, although some soldiers testified that anything prepared in mess halls left something to be desired. Most food was canned or freeze-dried and had been flown into the country from Germany. Fresh fruits and vegetables were nonexistent. Meals prepared in huge amounts lacked home-cooked flavor.

Soldiers work out at a makeshift gym assembled at the Kandahar base.

Army soldiers help themselves to a variety of dishes. Most military meals in Afghanistan lacked homemade flavor and freshness.

Despite the handicaps, menus were as varied as possible. Breakfasts could include scrambled eggs (made from powdered eggs), hash browns, French toast, and the like. Dinners ranged from meatballs and mixed vegetables to chicken patties and rice. Soldiers also continued to visit the PX where they could augment meals with pretzels, beef jerky, Pop Tarts, and other treats. Although beer was usually available on other army bases throughout the world, it was missing in Afghanistan in deference to Muslim law.

At rare intervals, military meals became holiday feasts. Thanksgiving and Christmas were celebrated with plenty of turkey, ham, pumpkin and apple pie, and ice cream. Troops were even treated to shrimp and cheesecake in some locales. "What's special about the menu is that these sailors can't get home to mama's pumpkin pie," said one cook aboard the USS *Constellation*, "so we've gotta provide mama's pie for them instead."[63]

A few American businesses provided welcome breaks in the mealtime routine as

"Send Me a DustBuster"

One of the most ever-present frustrations that all soldiers faced during their stay in Afghanistan was the dust, which threatened to smother everyone and everything. Journalist Martin Savidge briefly reports on the powdery irritant in an article titled "Please Send Me a DustBuster," found on the Internet at www.cnn.com.

When I awaken in the morning, the dust covers my face. My clothes are constantly dusty. Even the ones I zipped in my backpack. I shake the dust off them and wash it from me in a daily skirmish fought with a bucket and a bar of soap, feeling victorious when I turn to see that dust has settled onto my clothes while they were off my body. . . .

My teeth are gritty, i.e. dusty. The dust pours into me through my nose, my mouth, my food, even my drink. My water is dusty. Why it doesn't turn to mud, I can never figure.

well by sending their kitchens and/or their products into Afghanistan. For instance, in January 2002, Burger King shipped several "Burger Buses" equipped with broilers and condiment stations to locales in the war zone and began turning out thousands of Whoppers, BK Broilers, BK Big Fish, and cheeseburgers. In June 2002, the Outback Steakhouse, a chain of Australian-themed restaurants, donated dinners to the more than six thousand men and women stationed at Kandahar. The troops were able to enjoy rib-eye steaks, deep-fried Bloomin' Onions, and nonalcoholic beer. "They were so appreciative," said Dave Ellis, Outback's director of research and development. "Comfort is very hard to come by over there."[64]

Fit and Fighting

Comfort *was* hard to come by in Afghanistan, and disease was a threat to every soldier's comfort and good performance. Polio, hepatitis, whooping cough, cholera, and deadly fevers cropped up regularly in the native population. Influenza alone killed sixty Afghan children in early 2002, and forty people died that same year from Crimean Congo hemorrhagic fever, a viral infection that causes internal bleeding and liver and heart failure.

Soldiers were given a multitude of vaccinations before going overseas and were instructed to eat nothing but food provided by the military. Food given them by Afghan fighters or purchased from native bazaars could be dangerous. Medical personnel also knew that dust and dirt were perfect carriers for disease, and there was plenty of dust everywhere. "The first time I saw the dust in the air, I thought 'Oh my God, I'm going to get so sick'" said army captain D.J. Doyle, surgeon for the Eighty-second Airborne Division. "But it just hasn't happened."[65]

No epidemics of serious illness broke out in the first year, but doctors treated cases of malaria in troops who had been out in the field. The "Bagram bug," a viral infection characterized by fever and vomiting, sickened troops periodically, and more than one hundred soldiers at the Kandahar base fell ill after eating improperly prepared stuffing at Thanksgiving in 2001.

There were other health threats to be guarded against as well. Sunstroke and dehydration during hot days and hypothermia (subnormal body temperature) in the cold were real dangers. So were bites from carpet vipers, scorpions, and rats that were common to the region. Those men who fought in the mountains sometimes experienced altitude sickness, a condition resulting from quickly ascending to or descending from high altitudes. Symptoms included nausea, dizziness, headaches, and fatigue, but these usually faded away with time. "It's not a normal routine thing that we always have the opportunity to train our soldiers at high altitudes," said one training officer, Major Timothy Brooks. "One of the things we experienced during . . . battle is the change in temperature at high altitudes [as well]." [66]

Due to careful planning and instruction, few soldiers suffered from disease or disabilities while on deployment. And, although the danger remained real, most soldiers shrugged it off and went on with their work. "You can't let stuff like that get to you or you'll freak out and not be able to do your job," [67] said Airman Chris Higgins.

The Widespread Ailment

While physical illness was relatively rare, a great number of soldiers suffered from a different kind of malady—homesickness—while in Afghanistan. Many had babies at home who had been born after they were deployed and whom they had never seen. Many missed seeing toddlers walk for the first time, helping youngsters with homework, or attending school activities. One pilot, whose daughter had been crowned homecoming princess during his absence, mourned the fact that he had missed that special event. "Her swim coach is driving her around in my '65 'Vette [1965 Corvette]," he said. "God, how I wish I could be there!" [68]

Loneliness over the holidays was particularly difficult to combat. "This is my fourth Christmas in about five years away," notes Staff Sergeant David L. Smith. "Last year I was in Kosovo, the year before that Korea, and two years before that, Bosnia. I'd like to be able to watch them [my children] open presents. Nothing can replace that." [69]

The military tried to lessen the sadness by providing the best holiday celebrations it could. Meals were festive. Mess halls, especially those on carriers, were decorated with tinsel and lights. Troops sang Christmas carols and trimmed makeshift trees. Nevertheless, the mood for most men and women was melancholy. "For me it's just another day to get past before I get home," said Staff Sergeant Shamory Gipson, stationed at Bagram base. "I'm just going to ignore it and celebrate when I'm back with my family and friends. My mother told me to think of it as a growing experience." [70]

Despite the loneliness and isolation, most soldiers were well equipped to combat their feelings due to the advent of high-tech communications facilities. Letters from home were still a highlight of everyone's day, and military post offices worked overtime to ensure that packages and letters moved long distances as quickly as possible. More instantaneous communication was possible, however, because of e-mail and overseas telephone calls. Both helped tie families together across the miles. Bagram base alone was equipped with 250 computers for troop use, with diesel-powered generators to keep them running. "Most of the soldiers here use it [the Internet]," said Sergeant Jeffrey Franklin. "I e-mail my family to let 'em know . . . that I hadn't hit no land mine."[71]

Even soldiers who had little family support received letters, packages, and e-mails from concerned Americans including members of the Veterans of Foreign Wars,

Marines share family photos received in Christmas packages. Holidays are lonely for soldiers far from home.

Elks Club, and American Legion that helped ease loneliness. Gifts and notes from schoolchildren were especially appreciated. For instance, to show troops they cared, schoolchildren from Shoemaker Elementary in Gale City, Virginia, collected and sent packages filled with items such as Chapstick, shaving cream, toothpaste, shampoo, candy, and gum in February 2002. "We read several letters and articles about the soldiers and the conditions they were enduring in being away from home and separated from their families," explained teacher Kim Wilson who coordinated the project. "We told them [the students] this was a good way for us to help."[72]

Movies and Marathons

E-mails, letters, and telephone calls were prized, but they could not fill all the spare time soldiers had. Thus, most resorted to other meaningful or fun pastimes such as attending worship services, listening to music on CDs or radio, playing volleyball, or watching movies and football games on American Forces Television. Large numbers enjoyed broadcasts of the Super Bowl and the Salt Lake City Winter Olympics in the winter of 2002. Some members of the crew on aircraft carriers went swimming in the sea on warm days. Others entertained each other with karaoke or held mock sumo wrestling matches. Periodically, entertainers such as Drew Carey, Robin Williams, or David Letterman arrived to put on a show.

Some troops worked out or went for walks or runs. In an unusual move at Bagram base on Thanksgiving Day, 2002, a group of dedicated runners organized a twenty-six mile "Minefield Marathon" for those who enjoyed competitions. The name was chosen because the course was laid over cleared sections of a large minefield. "This was different than any other marathon . . . it was much more mentally challenging," said Lieutenant Ray Youngs who was the winner. "Here you don't get to train or eat the right way."[73]

One of the most unusual pastimes on Kandahar and Bagram bases was that of hunting for military treasures left over from the Soviet invasion. Equipment and supplies often littered base perimeters, giving treasure hunters the opportunity to find collectibles such as gauges, uniforms, belt buckles, and buttons. Those who hunted had to be alert for booby traps and hidden mines, but with care, an expedition could be rewarding. Journalist Martin Savidge reported during his visit to Kandahar base in early 2002, "I watch an Air Force crew walking back to their C-17 cargo jet with the rear rotor blades of another Russian war bird [helicopter]. . . . What will they do with them, I wonder? A ceiling fan? Or are they just destined to 'thingamabob' status, trading their Afghan dust for that found on some coffee table or desk?"[74]

Activities like treasure hunting, jogging, or e-mailing were important for troop well-being, but many soldiers found that their term of service did not allow for relaxation. For some, fighting the enemy was a fast and furious assignment. For others, it was a series of time-consuming but futile operations wherein Taliban and al-Qaeda fighters proved reclusive and difficult to catch. "It is the invisible enemy," observed one baffled Special Forces fighter, referring to the fact that adversaries slipped away or hid among innocent civilians. "It's the germ in the body. The body is sick, but how do you isolate the germ and kill it. It's frustrating."[75]

Chapter 4

In Pursuit of bin Laden

On September 20, 2001, President George W. Bush warned America that the war on terrorism would be a conflict unlike any other fought up to that time:

> Americans should not expect one battle, but a lengthy campaign, unlike any other we have ever seen. It may include dramatic strikes, visible on TV, and covert operations, secret even in success. We will starve terrorists of funding, turn them one against another, drive them from place to place, until there is no refuge or no rest. And we will pursue nations that provide aid or safe haven to terrorism. [76]

Americans could only imagine what the war would be like, but U.S. military men and women in Afghanistan knew firsthand the intensity of the struggle. They were on the ground, pursuing Taliban and al-Qaeda forces, intent upon carrying out

President Bush's determination to protect the United States from further incidents of terrorism.

Close Call

Bush had promised that some missions would be covert—carried out in secret— and one of the first of these, which took place early in the war, was almost a disaster for the special operations men involved. The details were not revealed to the public at the time, however, so few knew of the close call that had taken place near the city of Kandahar on October 20, 2001.

On that date, a group of soldiers made up of a Delta Force squadron and Army Rangers dropped into Afghanistan to carry out an assault on Mohammad Omar's compound and to try to catch the elusive Taliban leader. The residence was outside of Kandahar and was heavily fortified with high walls and a roof reinforced with tires and mud to withstand bombing. Although the Americans had been trained to attack quickly and quietly, their superiors chose to open the operation with barrages of bombs dropped by AC-130 gunship aircraft. The fighters doubted the wisdom of the approach, but true to their training, prepared to perform their part of the operation to the best of their abilities.

Immediately following the air assault, they stormed the compound. Inside, they did not find Omar or anything else of value. As they were leaving, however, Taliban forces, waiting in ambush, began firing rocket-propelled grenades at them. Some of the Americans were wounded, and the team had to retreat swiftly. "Don't put us in an environment we weren't prepared for," said one Delta Force soldier who was displeased by the less-than-perfect planning that went into the operation. "Next time, we're going to lose a company." [77]

The Air War

Covert operations aside, the war began much as Operation Desert Storm had in 1991—with a concentrated air campaign. On October 7, 8, and 9, dozens of U.S. and British planes began dropping their ordnance on Taliban missile and radar sites, airfields, motor pools, troop-training facilities, and al-Qaeda compounds. About fifty cruise missiles were launched from U.S. ships and British submarines as well. The capabilities of these ships, planes, and the explosives they delivered allowed targets to be hit with great precision.

During the next two months, the bombing campaign intensified. Flight crews began concentrating on hitting caves and tunnels in which al-Qaeda operatives hid and stored their weapons and munitions. The plan was to destroy as many of these mountain bunkers as possible, using a combination of conventional and unconventional bombs. Five-thousand-pound "bunker busting" bombs, which could penetrate up to twenty-two feet of earth and concrete before exploding, were employed. So were two-thousand-pound "thermobaric" bombs, which could suck air out of caves and suffocate those inside. Fifteen-thousand-pound "daisy cutter" bombs—the largest conventional bombs in existence—were also used with lethal effect.

The operations pushed crews to the limit. The missions did not involve simply flying over the site and dropping bombs. Hours of planning were required for each strike. Flight plans had to be studied and bomb runs memorized. Most runs originated from aircraft carriers or from the island of Diego Garcia, so planes had to fly hundreds of miles across Pakistan to reach their targets. A few crews flew from bases in the Persian Gulf and from air force bases in the United States, so they spent much longer in the air. Planes also spent five to nine hours over Afghanistan pounding their targets. (During Operation Desert Storm the aircraft did not spend more than three hours flying.) Pilots had to get special medical clearance to let them exceed the monthly limit of sixty-five hours of flight time.

By December 23, 2001, when sustained air operations slowed, more than 17,500

The colossal "daisy cutter" bomb blasted several Afghan targets with lethal force.

bombs and missiles had been dropped on or fired into Afghanistan. The United States had flown about sixty-five hundred strike missions—about two hundred sorties a day, with each bomber taking out an average of two targets. "A year ago, if I had been told we would be flying as intensely as we are right now . . . I would have said it might have broken the bank," said Captain Richard O'Hanlon, the USS *Roosevelt's* commanding officer. "It's been a test of endurance."[78]

Consummate Professionals

Those who made up the flight crews of the jets and bombers were highly skilled, highly motivated people who had risen to their positions through a combination of dedi-cation and hard work. Not only were they exceptional individuals, they had to interact as a team while they carried out their missions. "The aircraft are operated by some of the most specialized and unique airmen in the Air Force. . . . They spend most of their careers here. It takes a long time to train them."[79] said air force lieutenant Jeff Roberts, describing the AC-130 gunship crews.

Airmen also had to be at peace with the notion that the bombs they dropped every night killed people as well as destroyed inanimate objects. "When you deliver weapons, it's just a target. It's not about taking human life. It's about breaking their will to wage war,"[80] explained one pilot.

Nevertheless, with excellent technical and communications capabilities, it was not always easy to distance oneself from the

consequences of one's acts. In one instance, as bombs were dropped on Taliban troops, those in the plane were able to hear at least some of what went on below through radio contact with Special Forces on the ground. "We could hear the Northern Alliance troops cheering and celebrating over the radio,"[81] one flier noted.

Some of the newest aviators in the war were women pilots who for the first time were assigned to fly combat missions over Afghanistan. One of these women was Lieutenant Ashley (complete name withheld), stationed aboard the USS *Carl Vinson*.

One of fewer than one hundred American women to fly combat missions, a female navy pilot suits up before a bombing run.

Aware that she was one of fewer than one hundred women in what had once been an all-male world, she worked hard to be the complete professional who excelled on the job. "We [female pilots] are very few and far between but we just do our job like everyone else,"[82] she explained.

Ashley first flew a mission over Afghanistan in late October 2001 and remembered that her targets were two antiaircraft batteries. After hitting the first one, the enemy returned fire, sending gray puffs of smoke into the air. "I was excited and I was smiling because I had dropped my bombs and they had definitely hit,"[83] she remembered with satisfaction.

For all who fought from the air, dropping bombs to hit specific targets and miss innocent civilians was a challenging assignment. Those who released state-of-the-art smart bombs, which were guided to their targets by satellites, found that these munitions were more sensitive than more traditional bombs. And the task of programming smart bombs to hit targets close to Special Forces teams who called in the coordinates required extreme care. "It was

a new and different experience as a navigator and bombardier," said Major Bruce (complete name withheld). "Having to react to short-notice taskings, having guys on the ground relying on us to take the heat off of them . . . was more rewarding than anything we've done before."[84]

Even after completing a bombing run, pilots had to successfully make a landing, usually on aircraft carrier decks that were relatively confined. This was often the most dangerous part of the mission. The pilot had to touch down in exactly the right spot so that the plane's tailhook could catch one

An F-14 fighter jet makes a tricky landing on the deck of the USS Kennedy.

of four heavy wires strung across its path on the deck. Once hooked, the plane was jerked to a stop in just two hundred feet. The margin of error for hooking was only eighteen inches, however, and pilots always hit the throttle at the last minute so they could take off again if necessary.

Pilots sometimes compared the process to threading a needle while running across a room in the dark. When asked what he thought as he began his landing after a long run, one pilot said, "I say to myself, 'Please God, don't let me screw this up.'"[85]

A Unique Campaign

While pilots risked their lives in the air war that was being fought over Afghanistan, special operations teams took on the task of fighting the war on the ground. This aspect of the conflict was indeed unprecedented. In other wars, conventional forces had done most of the fighting, while Rangers, Green Berets, and others had provided specialized support. The opposite was true in Afghanistan. There, the bulk of the fighting was carried out by special ops, as they were nicknamed. One navy SEAL explained: "Up until March, this was a SOF [special-operations forces] campaign, supported by conventional forces. All our operations were SOF-specific. That didn't change until Operation Anaconda, when SOF shifted focus and began to support the conventional forces."[86]

The unique nature of the campaign allowed much of the planning and control of the war to be in the hands of comman-dos rather than more traditional commanders. Decisions were made quickly, on site, and from a more informed perspective. Forces could thus identify and eliminate enemy positions more efficiently.

The setup also allowed the navy to play a role that it might not ordinarily have assumed during war in a landlocked country such as Afghanistan. Navy SEALs—who were skilled in land as well as underwater missions—took part in many of the ground operations, and a SEAL commander, Captain Robert Harvard, commanded a task force made up of U.S. Army, Navy, and Air Force personnel, as well as forces from Australia, Denmark, Germany, Norway, and Turkey. "The Afghan campaign, its SOF leadership, its joint and coalition nature, its operational agility, and the premium it placed on accurate information—all of these qualities epitomize [characterize] the type of warfare that will be needed to subdue global terrorism,"[87] said Harvard.

Team Effort

The overall aim of special operations teams was to help the Northern Alliance overthrow the Taliban. One method of achieving this involved providing information to bomber squads about sites that should be targeted. At least one member of each team was a combat controller who was expert at guiding high-flying aircraft to targets using laser range finders, target designators, and powerful telescopes and radios. With their skills—and by coordinating with the crews of bombers and

Northern Alliance soldiers fire on the Taliban using howitzer cannons. Most Alliance forces carried only small weapons.

fighter jets overhead—they were able to help eliminate large groups of the enemy with deadly effect.

On November 10, 2002, in the first notable victory in the war, General Dostum's militia, with the help of Operational Detachment Alpha 595, was able to drive the Taliban out of the northern city of Mazār-e Sharīf. The Taliban were equipped with tanks, air-defense guns, mortars, and machine guns; the Alliance had nothing but small arms at their disposal. As the battle took shape, however, Alpha 595 divided into four teams in order to make the best use of their skills and their continued radio access to aerial firepower. They felt confident breaking into small groups because Dostum and his men were fierce fighters, willing to support and protect them. "We began to have this trust and rapport developed with certain key commanders that were in the mid-level range of his [Dostum's] commanders,"[88] explained one of the unit's members.

One team, coupled with Dostum's militia, worked to prevent Taliban reinforcements from coming to the city's aid, and another directed an air assault upon the Taliban's rear. The other two led a main frontal assault on the city. A member of one of the teams explained how, between bomb strikes, the ground war became one-on-one fighting at times. "Once they [Dostum's militia] closed with the Taliban, their technique can best be described as the swarm. They were at the gallop, firing their assault weapons. . . . And they would simply ride down any Taliban that attempted to resist. . . . And as they took these objectives, we would bring in the close air support again."[89]

In the process of the fighting, hundreds of enemy troops were killed, and thirty members of the Northern Alliance were lost. Nevertheless, the victory was a quick one as Taliban forces broke and ran for their lives. The effect was encouraging, and when asked if they felt they were avenging the events of September 11, one Special Forces operative observed, "Some of it was 'Yeah, these are bad guys that have done bad things to my country. They're going to get bad things in return.' But I didn't think of myself as an avenger. I thought of myself as a soldier doing my mission so that I can carry on with my next mission, which is to go home."[90]

Breaking the Taliban

American soldiers had expected that toppling the Taliban would take months, so they were pleased when the operations to break the regime's power moved ahead rapidly and with relative ease. Mazār-e Sharīf was only one of dozens of towns that they helped the Northern Alliance recapture in the fall and winter of 2001. Another significant takeover took place in early December, when anti-Taliban troops and American Special Forces fought together with Afghan leader Hamid Karzai and his supporters to bring about the surrender of Kandahar, birthplace of the Taliban and its spiritual headquarters. Special Forces operative captain Jason Amerine, fighting beside Karzai (who would be elected interim president of Afghanistan in December 2001), described the scene:

From November 17 until about the end of the month, for about two weeks, we'd be bombing things, securing the area, bringing in food, bringing in weapons— working on securing the area, with all sorts of coordinations. We were trying to figure out how and when to take Kandahar. I had a relatively conservative approach. I thought we probably should have an army before we try to take [it].[91]

Again, to everyone's surprise and relief, Taliban forces gave way as Karzai and the Americans moved closer to the city. Although Mohammad Omar fled, his followers soon agreed to surrender, and Northern Alliance forces entered Kandahar on December 8, 2001. The city had been the last Taliban stronghold, and with its fall, the radical Islamic government was removed from power. Amerine remembered their entry into the city. "We had a number of Taliban change sides. One minute you're shooting at them, and the next minute they are now your allies and your friends. . . . So it was just kind of an unnerving situation—one day they were my enemy, and the next day they're on my side and we're all heading towards Kandahar."[92]

Camps and Caves

After breaking the Taliban's grip on the cities and populated regions of Afghanistan, the focus of the war turned to the mountainous eastern parts of the country. Here Osama bin Laden and his al-Qaeda associates were believed to be hiding in caves and hideouts.

Despite the skill and efficiency of the Special Forces, the hunt for bin Laden proved to be a more baffling and time-consuming task than breaking the power of the Taliban. Hiding places were numerous, many residents of the area were sympathetic to the terrorists, and any Westerner took his life in his hands when he moved through the countryside. "They're really bad guys. If you look like an American they'll kill you,"[93] said one Special Forces operative by the name of "Mike."

Despite the danger, U.S. troops were regularly dropped into the region by helicopter. They then determinedly hiked across the rugged terrain or rode donkeys and horses for days to reach designated camps and caves. Intense bombing had destroyed many of the sites, cutting the risk that they would meet an army of well-armed terrorists as they made their searches. More often than not, they found the caves and compounds they came across abandoned. The enemy had received word of their approach and had fled.

Each locale was thoroughly searched, however, and anything of value was taken. Most of the hideouts contained only left-over boxes of ammunition or Arabic training manuals, but sometimes there were shooting targets, packages of food such as dates, pieces of clothing, or exercise equipment such as parallel bars.

One of the largest camps, Rish Khor, in the mountains south of Kabul, proved to be an exception in that it was a veritable treasure trove of documents and weapons. Searchers going into it in late 2001 found instructions on military tactics, information on booby traps and bomb making, switches, and weapons manuals. They found dozens of personnel files complete with photos and biographical sketches of each man. There were also notes on chemistry and physics—presumably to aid in the manufacture of bombs.

In April 2002, American troops were able to access the Zhawar Kili camp near the city of Khowst in eastern Afghanistan. This, too, was a rich source of valuable material. The huge complex, made up of fifty caves, eleven tunnels, and more than sixty

Navy SEALs search through boxes of ammunition stashed in one of the caves at the abandoned Zhawar Kili camp.

buildings, covered a nine-square-mile area and included an arms depot, repair shops, a radio center, a medical clinic, a hotel, and a mosque. Al-Qaeda had used the camp as a logistics base, a command and control center, and a training ground. "We saw . . . unbelievable cave complexes," one man testified. "It was mind-boggling how far they go into the mountains."[94]

Inside the camp, the Americans found countless al-Qaeda intelligence documents, as well as cell phones, laptop computers, and nearly a million pounds of hidden weapons and munitions. After gathering up anything of importance, they called in air support to ensure the destruction of the refuge. "We wanted to deny al-Qaida and the Taliban the chance to regroup, certainly the chance to rebuild their logistical infrastructure. And [we wanted] to continue the destruction of al-Qaida forces,"[95] said Major Ignacio Perez, a 101st Airborne spokesman.

American troops had hoped to corner Osama bin Laden and Mohammad Omar in the caves of Afghanistan, so the failure to find and capture them was disappointing. On February 14, 2002, however, they were able to apprehend a high-ranking Taliban official, Mullah Khairullah Kahirkawa, who was hiding in the same region. The mullah, who was the former governor of the city of Herat and a close associate of Omar, had taken refuge near the Pakistan border, and there he was spotted by one of America's unmanned Predator drones, used to provide photo surveillance in the area. Intent on capturing Kahirkawa, navy

SEALs landed by helicopter in the dead of night and surrounded the fugitive. His capture took place with relative ease, and he was then flown off to an undisclosed location.

Operation Anaconda

American troops found it easier to cope with loneliness, disappointment, and rough living conditions when successful operations such as the capture of Mullah Kahirkawa took place. Missions such as Operation Anaconda, which occurred in the spring of 2002, however, made their terms of service seem almost unbearably difficult.

Chopper Assignment

Chinook helicopter pilots were some of the most valuable, and most fearless, fighters in the war. In "First Wave: The Soldiers' Story," pilots Scott Breslin and John W. Quinlan recalled a few moments of dropping troops off for Operation Anaconda, one of the most dangerous battles of their careers. More of their story can be read on the Internet at http://abcnews.go.com.

Chief Warrant Officer 3 Scott Breslin, Chinook pilot: "[We were] actually enjoying some of the scenery. It sounds crazy, but it's really pretty country that we're flying over here. Until you get to that last couple of minutes, it's kind of an enjoyable flight."

.... As the Chinooks dropped off the troops, [however] they came under heavy fire almost immediately....

Quinlan: "Immediately on the ground, those guys were pinned down. The al Qaeda was firing down off the mountains into the valley and the situation was developing. But we

had another turn to make. We had to bring more infantry guys in...."

Breslin: "I realized it's not a training mission any more. There's really people that are shooting at us, or at least at the helicopter."

... Choppers continued to fly missions to drop troops off, until they were prevented from doing so, as the battle heated up.... By nightfall, 18 hours after the first troops had been inserted, they received orders to extract them. Pilots began flying out wounded and exhausted soldiers as Air Force bombers bombarded the caves. Eight U.S. soldiers were killed during Anaconda.

Quinlan: "... We know a lot of those guys. And the special operations guys we've worked with in the past as well, so it was— you don't like to hear about a brother getting hurt or someone getting killed like that. No one wants to hear that.... You don't leave a soldier behind."

Operation Anaconda, named for a non-poisonous snake that kills its prey by squeezing, was a "mop-up" operation meant to surround, corner, and annihilate remaining pockets of al-Qaeda and Taliban who hid in the mountains of Afghanistan. U.S. commanders estimated that it would be a short operation; some hoped it would be complete in twenty-four hours. Their optimism would be short-lived.

On March 2, 2002, Chinook helicopters began to deposit U.S. troops—among them navy SEALs, Special Forces, and members of the Tenth Mountain Light Infantry Division—into position. All had been trained to fight in rugged terrain and were well prepared for an operation that would take place at altitudes above eight thousand feet, on rocky ground covered with snow, where temperatures dropped below freezing at night.

Despite well-laid plans, as the fighters stepped out of their helicopters, they realized that the enemy was more numerous and more aggressive than had been expected. Chief Warrant Officer John W. Quinlan, a helicopter pilot, remembered what took place as he dropped off his load of troops. "Immediately on the ground, those guys were pinned down. The al-Qaeda was firing down off the mountains into the valley and the situation was developing. But we had another turn to make. We had to bring more infantry guys in. We had to get our helicopters back here to Bagram to do the next infiltration."[96]

Not only were there four times as many enemy fighters as expected, they were well

"I'm Not Going to Die"

In an article titled "Soldier Recounts Fateful Operation Anaconda Battle," published in the Knight-Ridder/Tribune News Service, journalist John Gittelsohn describes Sergeant Robert Mc-Cleave's brush with death during one of the most dangerous clashes in the war.

Just as McCleave's unit decided to run for cover, a shell landed a few feet behind him. "It felt like 10 people came at me with baseball bats and hit me at the same time," he said. . . . Fear and adrenaline carried McCleave to cover in a dry riverbed, a spot later dubbed "Hell's Halfpipe" because it looked like a snowboarding chute. He was surrounded by other wounded men awaiting evacuation. . . . Sometimes McCleave glimpsed al-Qaida soldiers, men in black robes who seemed to be shooting. They were far away and disappeared whenever American helicopters or planes attacked. But the mortars kept coming, and shrapnel hit him again in mid-afternoon. . . .

"I was thinking I'm not going to die in Afghanistan," he said. "I was thinking, when I die, it's going to be somewhere in California and I'll be old and I'll have seen my daughter grow up and see her kids and see them have kids and maybe even see them have kids."

It was 11 P.M., 15 hours after he left Bagram [his home base], when a Chinook [helicopter] finally came to evacuate McCleave. Of the 86 men in his unit, 28 were wounded, but none died and no one was left behind.

entrenched and well armed with mortars and heavy machine guns. Lieutenant Joe Harosky, second platoon commander, remembered, "We had initially thought it [the firing] wasn't directed at us or a company. So I just kept walking in a normal speed, thinking hey, the firing is on the other side of a mountaintop or ridge."[97]

It did not take long for Harosky and the rest to realize that they were involved in an extremely tough battle. For days they fought the enemy, making little significant headway. On March 4, eight U.S. soldiers were killed. One fell from a helicopter that was fired upon by rocket-propelled grenades, and seven others died while engaged in an hour-long gunfight with al-Qaeda forces. The fact that hundreds of al-Qaeda were reported killed during the interaction did not make American losses any easier to accept.

In the end, Operation Anaconda lasted more than two weeks and involved one thousand U.S. troops, plus Afghan fighters and coalition forces from countries like Canada and Australia. On March 18, the operation was finally declared complete, although troops remained in the mountains to continue looking for enemy fighters who had escaped. Neither Osama bin Laden, Mullah Omar, nor any other top al-Qaeda operatives had been captured or killed. The dubious ending caused some to question whether the mission had been a victory or not. Nevertheless, General Tommy Franks offered his congratulations to the participants. "You did it, you did it on time, you did it with a good plan, you did it with violent execution, you did it taking care of one another,"[98] he noted.

KIA and Friendly Fire

Despite battles like Operation Anaconda and ever-present danger that American soldiers faced elsewhere throughout Afghanistan, casualties were few in the war. By the end of 2002, just over fifty men had been killed and less than three hundred injured in accidents and hostile incidents.

Although all soldiers accepted the risk of death as part of their job descriptions, even the loss of one person was distressing. The most publicized was that of Johnny Micheal "Mike" Spann, a thirty-two-year-old marine who served as an officer in the Central Intelligence Agency (CIA). Spann was in Mazār-e Sharīf, questioning captured Taliban fighters, when the prisoners unexpectedly pulled out weapons and staged a revolt inside the prison. During the uprising, Spann was killed—the first American to be killed in action (KIA) in Afghanistan. "This was a guy we considered part of our unit," explained a Special Forces captain who wanted to be known only as Mark. His grief over the incident was apparent. "If we had been there, Mike's death would not have happened."[99]

Just as upsetting to troops were incidents of "friendly fire," so called because attacks came not from the enemy but from fellow soldiers who had somehow mistaken their targets. On November 26, 2001, five Special Forces men were wounded near Mazār-e Sharīf when a bomb was mistakenly

Marine Corps honor guards carry the body of CIA officer Micheal Spann, the first American killed in action in Afghanistan.

programmed to hit their position instead of the planned target. Over a week later, on December 4, three Special Forces soldiers and seven Afghans were killed by friendly fire near Kandahar. "That obviously was the worst day of the war for us, for me and for all of our 5th Group, where we lost three soldiers and many Afghan counterparts. [We] basically lost the entire A-team to wounds,"[100] said Colonel John Mulholland, who was commander of the unit that was targeted.

Incidents involving the deaths of civilians from friendly fire were just as troubling as military casualties. One such death occurred when a Red Cross compound in Kabul was accidentally targeted in October 2001. In July 1, 2002, members of a wedding celebration in northern Afghanistan were injured and killed after the weapons they were shooting in celebration were mistaken for enemy gunfire. The military was quick to express its regrets for all the incidents, but also pointed out that accidents were bound to occur in war. "These are human-made, human-designed systems, and therefore, they're going to have flaws that are going to either be built in or that are going to occur. We have not perfected a technology that is perfect in its execution,"[101] stated Rear Admiral John Stufflebeem.

Although most instances of friendly fire were accepted as part of war, at least one incident that occurred in April 2002 was not. During that month, two pilots in a U.S. F-16 fighter plane dropped a bomb on Canadian soldiers conducting a night patrol near Kandahar. Four of them were killed. An inquiry later in the year recommended that disciplinary action be taken against the pilots, who had disobeyed orders when they dropped the bomb.

Guerrilla Warfare

Incidents of friendly fire and qualified successes such as Operation Anaconda were examples of the imperfect state of affairs that American soldiers faced as the war approached its one-year anniversary. Osama bin Laden, Omar, and many of their associates had mysteriously vanished. Members of the Taliban—most of them native Afghans—had slipped away into Pakistan or resumed their lives as ordinary citizens and so could not be found. "They can hide and come back anytime they want,"[102] observed one Special Forces soldier who preferred to be called "Oklahoma Chris."

The war slowed to a series of skirmishes— "hard-core guerrilla warfare"[103] in the words of one soldier. Small, heavily armed patrols that tried to flush out those who hid in the hills coped almost daily with rocket fire and hit-and-run attacks from unseen foes. These assaults could be deadly. In August 2002, one soldier died after being ambushed and shot. Another was killed when his unit was involved in a sudden firefight near the Pakistan border. "It suggests that

Unforgettable Decision

Lieutenant Colonel David L. Fox was the commander responsible for calling in a smart bomb drop that took the lives of three American soldiers on December 4, 2001. Fox or one of his men had changed a dead battery on their Global Positioning System device immediately before calling in the coordinates, unaware that the device automatically reset to its own position. Fox's interview with *Frontline,* part of "Campaign Against Terror," can be found on the Internet at www.pbs.org.

The first thing is that I think about those three soldiers every day. There's not a day that goes by that I don't think about Master Sergeant Jeff Davis, Staff Sergeant Dan Petithory and Staff Sergeant Cody Prosser. I think about them, I miss them, they were great soldiers, great Americans, and they were doing what they loved. So you never forget. This past Memorial Day was especially tough and July 4. . . .

[Question:] Do you ever second-guess and think, "Maybe I shouldn't have called in the strikes that day?"

Every day. I second-guess every decision, especially when one of my soldiers gets hurt or gets injured, or even one of the Afghan soldiers. "Could I have done it better? Is there something I forgot? Was everything in place?" I think about it and I second-guess myself every day. I'm sure that there was something I could have done better. There was something I could have done to prevent it. . . . But it's just something I'm going to have to live with for the rest of my life.

we're facing a committed enemy," Colonel Roger King, a military spokesman, said. "It suggests what we've tried to say all along, that this is not a quick fix, it's not going to be over tomorrow. It will be a long drawn-out campaign." [104]

Left with a hard-to-find adversary, U.S. troops had no choice but to persist in what often seemed like a hopeless task. They were well supported in that task by thousands of military men and women who—

though many never took up arms in pursuit of the enemy—were nevertheless as committed to success as any frontline soldier. And, although they did not share the glory with the fighters, they were indispensable to every mission. "Everybody wants us. Everybody needs us," said one engineer, speaking for all those who provided backup in the war. "Everybody knows we can make life a lot easier. They know what we bring to the fight." [105]

Chapter 5

Behind the Scenes

By early January 2002, a total of four thousand ground troops had been deployed to Afghanistan. At the end of August, the numbers had swollen to eight thousand. More than half of these were "logistics" workers, those who were in charge of acquiring, maintaining, and transporting people, equipment, and everything else used in a war. These behind-the-scenes forces—engineers, medics, cooks, clerks, and a host of others—were seldom seen on nightly news reports. Still, as Major Steve Larsen, executive officer for the Ninety-second Engineer Battalion pointed out, "A professional soldier knows no one person makes a war happen. . . . All of the folks who go unsung are critical."[106]

On the Ground, on the Sea

Support personnel made up most of the population on the many carriers and ships involved in the war. Along with clerks, maintenance workers, and technicians, one hundred and fifty cooks prepared about twenty thousand meals per day on the USS *Carl Vinson* alone. Ten barbers gave about twenty-five thousand haircuts during a six-month cruise. Two surgeons, four doctors, and seventy-five medical corpsmen serviced a facility that included a fully equipped operating room. A psychologist was available to minister to everyone's mental and emotional needs. "There are [about] 5,500 people on an aircraft carrier," said Lieutenant Helen Napier, one of the first psychologists to serve on a carrier. "The average age is about 19, so you are dealing with a lot of 'adjustment to life' situations. For many of these Sailors, it's their first time away from home, and we'll be gone through all the major holidays. That takes a toll."[107]

On bases in Afghanistan as well, thousands of logistics workers served day and night to keep operations running smoothly. Cooks prepared thousands of meals. Clerks ensured that paychecks were delivered, mail was distributed, and everything from pencils to ammunition was ordered and on

A military policewoman keeps a sharp lookout on her watch at Bagram Air Base.

hand. Public works teams took care of stringing communications wires, establishing garbage dumps and pickup service, and other similar tasks. Military Police (MPs) patrolled and enforced security and also served as guards for prisoners who awaited processing.

While many MPs remained on base, others went out on local reconnaissance patrols to learn of any enemy threat in the immediate area. In the southern part of the country, three American female MPs provided a unique form of service as they patrolled with infantrymen. Their assignment was to help in sensitive situations such as searches when Afghan women were involved. The three MPs were treated with great respect by the infantrymen they accompanied, but in a male-dominated nation, they drew curious and sometimes outraged stares from Afghans. "The men and kids are shocked to see us carry a weapon," remarked Sergeant Stephanie Blazo, "but we haven't had trouble with them so far." [108]

"Doing Your Part"

In addition to cooks, clerks, and MPs, there were hundreds of men and women on bases and carriers who directly supported the aircraft that flew missions. Maintenance personnel serviced the planes. Refueling teams filled fuel tanks. Signalmen coordinated the takeoff and landing of helicopters and jets. Messengers constantly communicated with the officer of the deck, flight deck team leader, signalmen, and control tower to coordinate takeoffs and landings.

Munitions experts unloaded, unpacked, and transported components of bombs to assembly crews. These crews worked in small, secure rooms below deck, installing fuses, tail assemblies, and arming lanyards (nose, or nose and tail) to make the bombs mission-ready. When asked how he felt about his role as a bomb builder, Airman Brandon (last name withheld) was somewhat ambivalent.

"It's My Plane"

Although jet pilots had full responsibility for their planes while flying over Afghanistan, crewmen who ensured the craft's flightworthiness shared a feeling of possessiveness. Saul Ingle details the case of Michael Holmes in "'It's My Plane': A Brown Shirt At War," published in *All Hands* magazine.

When Airman Michael Holmes finally gets to his rack [bed] at the end of a long day of work on board USS *Carl Vinson*, he pauses for a moment and thinks. . . . Holmes is a plane captain assigned to VFA-94. "It's my plane," said Holmes, "until the pilot comes out [on the flight deck]. Then I give him a salute and turn it over."

Holmes is not only in charge of the most visible Hornet [fighter jet] in his squadron, he is also the leading airman of his shop. . . . In addition to being in charge of all the plane captains in his shop, he is also responsible for the accountability of every tool. "If one tool is missing, we have to stop all launches until we find it," said Holmes. "A missing tool is dangerous, because it means there's a chance it was left inside an aircraft. If that's the case it could compromise the mission and the life of the pilot and flight deck personnel, not to mention the taxpayer's investment in a multi-million dollar warplane."

[Every day] he makes his way to the steaming flight deck, where he takes a walk around the jet looking for any abnormalities. Opening panels, wiping down the canopy, checking air intakes and inspecting the landing gear, he is meticulous in his inspection.

After he has gone over the plane with a fine-tooth comb, he waits for the arrival of the pilot. . . . "I'm the happiest man on earth when I see the pilot, because when that plane takes off, I'm done," says Holmes.

"You feel bad in sort of a sense," he said, "but then you're doing your part for your country, too. I'm sure nobody in here wants to kill people. But you got to do what you got to do. If we don't do anything, it [terrorism] is going to get worse."[109]

After the bombs were built, other men and women loaded them into the planes. While the bombing campaign was underway, teams readied more than twelve thousand general-purpose, smart, cluster, and other types of bombs over the course of several weeks. "When a jet came back with no bombs, you realized what you did was history in the making and you were part of the war," said one weapons loader. "All the bombs were gone, the crew was pumped up with adrenaline. . . . You wanted to do it again."[110]

Airlifts and Air Cargo

While hundreds of men and women supported the machines that flew missions over

Munitions experts carefully load a bomb onto a fighter jet on the deck of an aircraft carrier.

Afghanistan, hundreds more piloted huge transport planes full of soldiers, equipment, supplies, ammunition, and fuel. Such cargo could not be moved efficiently into the land-locked country except by air. During the first six months of the war, the air force flew nearly forty-eight hundred airlift missions totaling about one hundred thousand hours of flight time. The missions moved more than sixty-four thousand passengers and more than one hundred and twenty-five thousand tons of cargo onto bases such as Bagram, Kandahar, Camp Rhino, and others.

Because the flights were extremely long and active-duty air personnel could fly only limited periods of time without rest, the air force soon found that it needed extra support. "In the beginning, we were flying so much that our crews were running out of flying time at an alarming rate,"[111] said Lieutenant Colonel Peter A. Herneise, commander of the Seventeenth Expeditionary Airlift Squadron (EAS).

To ease the problem, reservists who were experienced pilots were called up to do the job. They were mixed in with regular flight crews, often bringing a level of maturity and flight experience that younger pilots might lack. "We run about six to 13 missions a day," explained Lieutenant Colonel Joseph S. Heirigs, the EAS's director of operations. "The Reserve crews tend to be 50 to 60 percent of our assigned manpower. Using volunteer Reserve aircrews and support personnel has been an overwhelming success to this operation."[112]

For the first months of the war, airlifts in and out of bases occurred only at night in order to avoid possible enemy attacks during takeoff and landing. "We worked only in blackout operations," said Master Sergeant Todd Kuzia who was in charge of operations on the ground in Afghanistan. "But [we] got the job done and nobody got hurt."[113]

With the danger and the volume of traffic, planes landed, unloaded, and took off again as quickly as possible. Approximately thirty cargo deliveries per day took place at Bagram by March 2002. Base ground crews responsible for off-loading, refueling, maintenance, and the like had to be quick and efficient in order to prevent accidents or delays. As the danger of attack lessened, operations became round-the-clock and were even more stressful. "You have to stay loose," said Kuzia, who relied on humor when the tension got too high. "It's key to getting the job done here."[114]

Midair Refueling

Another nonstop service provided by support crews was that of midair refueling. Without the services of a tanker plane—a modified Boeing 707 carrying thousands of gallons of jet fuel—bombers and fighter jets would not have been able to remain long hours in the air, and many combat missions would have been impossible. As one airman says, "We provide the legs, to carry the muscle, to deliver the punch."[115]

Refueling in midair was no easy task. "You're talking about a plane that's half the size of a football field and he's going to pull up within 30 feet of us,"[116] says Airman Joey Myers, referring to one of the C-17 cargo jets they refueled. The plane to be refueled had to align itself under the tanker, match its speed, then hold steady while a flying boom (an aerial fuel hose) was lowered and locked into place. Fuel transferred through the boom at a rate of up to one thousand gallons per minute, but even then both planes had to maintain their positions for more than five minutes before the operation was complete. Turbulence or a miscalculation could result in scraped paint, a dent, or something worse. "This is not an easy job, but it is also not back-breaking. There can be a lot of pressure and stress when things don't seem to go your way. Attention to detail is a must when performing your duties, just as it is in many military professions, one wrong move can be fatal,"[117] says one female in-flight refueler.

Because aerial refueling was so important, and because the skill of the tanker operators made the operation possible, tanker crews were some of the most-valued support teams in the war. "Fighter jocks buy drinks for tanker crews, not the other way around,"[118] stated one tanker pilot.

"We Build, We Fight"

Among the most hardworking support teams on bases in Afghanistan were the Naval Mobile Construction Battalions, more commonly known as the Seabees, and the U.S. Army Engineers. These teams, some of the first to be deployed on the ground, focused on improving conditions at bases such as Camp Rhino, Bagram, and Kandahar through a variety of repair and construction operations. The Seabee motto, "We Build, We Fight," highlighted the fact that these skilled work-

---

Boom Operator

The assignment of boom operator on midair refueling missions is not reserved solely for men anymore. The account of one female operator who describes her job can be found on the Internet at www.militarywoman.org.

> I could not ask for a better job. I love this job, it is very exciting and gives off an unbelievable rush. . . . A Boom Operator's flying day is very long and even though you may be on a cargo haul, there is no time for sleep. Not only does a Boom refuel aircraft in the air, but they also handle passengers, somewhat like a flight attendant (but we don't like to be called that), load cargo, we are another set of eyes for the pilots (we back them up). We basically have to know all of the systems on the aircraft just in case something goes wrong, we should be able to respond with the knowledge of what is going on. A typical day lasts anywhere between 10–16 hours, and by the time that day is over, you are pretty much exhausted, but it's worth it.

> There are a lot of perks that come with this job. I have seen a lot of the world, and I'm not just talking about seeing bases. . . . Incentive pay is always a plus, and having two officers take you to work everyday while you lay on your stomach and "pass gas" is a great way to earn your pay. I guess if you like to travel, this is a great job. I am happy to be serving my country and doing the job that I do.

Navy Seabees in Kandahar construct a detainee shelter for captured Taliban soldiers.

ers were also prepared to defend themselves in dangerous, unsecured areas.

Because bases were entirely dependent on cargo planes to provide the necessities of life, the Seabees' first missions were always runway repair and maintenance. Within days of their arrival, runways and taxiways were cleared of dangerous debris and bomb craters were filled with concrete. "The first one [crater] was done with one 11-cubic-foot mixer; that took 22 hours to complete from beginning to end. It took about 40 batches of concrete using the smaller mixer,"[119] remembers Lieutenant Donald Panthan, a

Seabee reservist called to active duty in Kandahar in late September 2001.

Other projects followed in quick succession. To keep dust down in the camps, the men spread tons of gravel. They helped construct walls and guard towers. They strung electric wires, repaired wells, and installed a portable helicopter landing pad. They also took their turns standing security patrols with other units. "We continue to make a difference and put another place in history for the 'Can Do' spirit of the Seabees," says Panthan. "Everyone has been putting in long hours and at times we have felt exhaustion, but we support each other and together we have pulled through. We are very proud to have had the opportunity to turn 'Can Do' into 'Have Done.'"[120]

Water in the Desert

In a drought-stricken country, providing water to thousands of troops was a top priority, and, at first, everyone made do with very little of the precious liquid. Bottled drinking water had to be airlifted into the country.

At Bagram, support crews made locating a water source a top priority. "Flying water in was expensive and cumbersome," explained Lieutenant Colonel Lonzel Lakey. "Bottled water took up lots of space that could have gone to other critical needs. We needed a natural clean drinking water source."[121] A nearby river was too polluted to be safely used, but a little exploration uncovered a forgotten well that the Soviets had dug in the 1980s. After cleaning and repair of the generator and pump, a stream of clear water came gushing out, ready to be chlorinated and used. The supply was ample for both the needs of the base and for local villagers to use as well. "It's a great feeling to succeed in getting something that's badly needed by your soldiers, while at the same time helping some people who have been suffering for a long time,"[122] stated Major Monte Yoder, a support operations officer.

At the Kandahar base, a demand for twenty-five thousand gallons of water per day for drinking, showers, and other activities, caused officials to bring in a Reverse Osmosis Purification Unit (ROPU). Local water was making troops sick, and the process successfully filtered out even the tiniest of impurities. "Water is not a glamour thing, or a high profile thing—but the minute we turn it off, you bet it is. Nobody cares until the water is gone,"[123] said Sergeant Mark Pennie, a Canadian water and environmental technician.

Laundries on bases were dependent on water and laundry support units who manned the facilities. They found that washing clothes was a never-ending chore. Every day, they worked with huge bags of dusty uniforms, feeding them into industrial-sized washing machines, then drying them and returning them to their owners. "Make no mistake," says Lieutenant Brian Manguel, who operated one of the laundries. "We're in the business of cleaning soldiers. They were all smiles when we showed up."[124]

Danger UXO

The Explosive Ordnance Disposal (EOD) unit performed another invaluable service. They worked together with other groups to rid bases and surrounding areas of thousands of unexploded bombs, mortar rounds, and land mines, known as UXO (unexploded ordnance).

The devices were virtually everywhere; Afghanistan was believed to be among the top five most heavily mined places in the world. One mine was discovered next to a bathroom, another near the Bagram base headquarters. In some regions, unexploded cluster bombs were clearly visible and littered the fields for a half-square-mile area. In other locales, mines were buried in the ground, and came to the surface only after it rained. Some mines were small, designed to maim or kill anyone who stepped on them. Others were powerful enough to destroy a tank.

Faced with the danger, the EOD unit carried out some missions by running a detonation cord to each mine or bomb they found and then detonating it. Norwegian bomb tcams, who soon arrived to help with demining, opted to use a device called a flail. This was an armored truck with a rotating tool on the front made of heavy chains. Put in motion, the chains pulverized the ground, stirring up a cloud of dirt and setting off any bomb they hit.

Beginning in January 2002, a private demining firm, Ronco Consulting Corp., based in Washington, D.C., was hired by the U.S. State Department to work in Afghanistan. In addition to using flails, it used dogs

Ordnance disposal specialists carefully detonate unexploded munitions abandoned by al-Qaeda.

that were specially trained to sniff out hidden explosives. "The dogs are trained to smell explosives, but it's sort of like smelling perfumes. There are just so many kinds," [125] says Fred Eastall, who led the Ronco team.

With thousands of mines to sniff out, the dogs and their handlers worked seven days a week, from 4 A.M. until 11 A.M. Early mornings were best to avoid the heat and human and vehicle traffic. Working in a small area, the handler kept his animal on a leash but allowed it to range and smell the ground thoroughly. When the dog detected an explosive, it sat. The handler, clad in heavy gear with a plastic face shield an inch thick, then investigated the area and marked the mine for later removal.

As of June 2002, almost 570,000 square meters (140 acres) of ground had been cleared in Afghanistan, with hundreds of thousands of mines and unexploded ordnance found. No dogs were killed or injured in the demining efforts, but there were at least six human casualties. Army Major Rod, an engineer who coordinated the demining program and did not want his full name used, could not ignore the danger. "My family knows I'm here, but they don't know what I'm doing. I don't want to worry them." [126]

"I Can Save Lives"

In the midst of so much danger, medical teams who oversaw the health and well-being of troops overseas were also vital to the war effort. Every Special Forces team included a medical sergeant who was trained to care for the wounded. However, if injuries

---

Front Line of Terror

After letters contaminated with anthrax sickened and killed several Americans in the fall of 2001, working in the mail room of the USS *Carl Vinson* required as much courage as stepping on a battlefield. Saul Ingle's article "The New Front Line," published in *All Hands* magazine, explains that all postal clerks took the threat seriously.

Postal Clerk Third Class Eric Gomez works in the mailroom on board USS *Carl Vinson*, which played a major role in the opening days of Operation Enduring Freedom. [The ship's crew] were not only fighting terror over Afghanistan, but in the ship's post office as well. With worries about the possibility of anthrax being sent through the mail, Gomez and the rest of *Vinson*'s PCs [postal clerks] stepped up safety precautions for moving the carrier's mail, much like their counterparts back home.

"We get suspicious packages every day," said the San Diego native. "Most of the time it's just melted chocolate or shampoo, but we check anyway. . . ."

To protect against the threat of anthrax during deployment, the PCs on *Vinson* wore gloves and masks while handling the mail. There have also been changes in the sorting process. "We handle the mail a lot more carefully," said Gomez.

In a war against terror, communicating by mail while at sea is just another reason for postal clerks, and other Sailors, to be ever vigilant in protecting that freedom.

were numerous, serious, or extensive, Special Forces operatives transferred the injured as quickly as possible to forward surgical teams, successors to Mobile Army Surgical Hospital (MASH) units of the Korean and Vietnam Wars. Made up of twenty members including doctors, nurses, surgeons, and technicians, these surgical teams were commonly located on bases. Sometimes, however, they positioned themselves in areas where battles were actually taking place.

Forward surgical teams performed emergency surgeries and treated everything from gunshot wounds to appendicitis. Another of their primary missions was to stabilize severely wounded patients before they were airlifted to facilities where they could receive more complete care. Such destinations were usually a base in Uzbekistan or further west at Landstuhl Regional Army Hospital in Landstuhl, Germany. The latter was the biggest U.S. military medical facility in Europe. Critical care air-transport teams, who were equipped to care for patients suffering from shock, bleeding, and respiratory failure, always accompanied those who were airlifted.

The men and women who served on various medical teams in Afghanistan were highly skilled and able to work under pressure when conditions were less than favorable. Many were reservists. In contrast to earlier wars, many of the nurses who served on the teams were male, attracted to military nursing because of the travel opportunities, because they could take leadership

roles, and because of the adventure. "I can do the he-man stuff in the military," says army nurse Major Michael Sadler. "I can go into battle with special operations soldiers and get shot at. I wear a uniform with patches and medals that say I'm tough, too; and what's more, I can save lives every day." [127]

Although all such medical personnel focused primarily on treating Americans who were sick and wounded, they did not hesitate to help Afghan fighters, even if these were enemy prisoners. All prisoners were seen by doctors who gave them the best available medical care. Those prisoners who were sent to Camp X-Ray, a holding facility at the U.S. Navy base at Guantánamo Bay, Cuba, were treated there for tuberculosis, malaria, frostbite, pneumonia, and any other conditions they had acquired. "Yes they're detainees, but they're also patients, and they are going to receive the same type of quality care that military folks would receive," [128] says Chief Bill Austin, public affairs officer at the camp hospital at Guantánamo Bay.

Guarding the Enemy

While medical teams tended to the health of Taliban and al-Qaeda captives, other troops were given the task of guarding them. A disastrous November 25, 2001, prison uprising near the city of Mazār-e Sharīf that resulted in the death of Micheal Spann and hundreds of Afghans provided a grim reminder that conditions for prisoners—both in Afghanistan and elsewhere—had to be

Two Camp X-Ray guards escort a prisoner as inmates watch from their cells at Guantánamo Bay, Cuba.

extremely secure. "You don't know if they're terrorists, you don't know, really who they are," said one guard who often escorted detainees for questioning. "So we treat everybody as potential killers at any moment for our safety."[129]

Most detainees were held at Bagram and Kandahar bases, although hundreds were transferred to Camp X-Ray in Cuba. In all locales, facilities were clean and humane, but virtually escape-proof. All were surrounded by coils of barbed wire, topped with watchtowers, and well lit twenty-four hours a day. Each detainee was held in a separate cell and was checked by regular roving patrols.

Shifts for guards were short so that they remained fresh and alert. Those who served food; took detainees to showers; or admitted doctors, chaplains, or Red Cross workers worked in teams and watched the prisoners closely. Continuous vigilance was a necessity because detainees often threatened to kill their guards, and one unwary guard was attacked and bitten. Even repeated searches of the men occasionally yielded razors and other sharp objects.

"Given the chance, they would hurt you or me," said Sergeant Eric Bokinsky.[130]

Despite the stress and thanklessness of their task, all who served as guards believed the job they were doing was worthwhile. Nevertheless, feelings about their assignment were mixed. "This is a big learning experience for me," said Specialist Rochelle Williams, a supply clerk who helped make sure each detainee received his allotted bedding, towels, and toiletries. "We're putting our lives on the line to take care of them when they'll do anything they can to kill us."[131] Sergeant Robert Wood, a national guardsman who served at Guantánamo was more objective. "I'm not here to judge. I can't let my feelings come into play about what crimes they've committed. I can't take it personal. I have to be a professional."[132]

Whether prison guard or tanker crew, military support personnel realized that they would never receive the acclaim and the admiration given to those who fought on the front lines. Nevertheless, they reminded themselves that the war was a team effort and that their work was important and interesting. The war was progressing, and the lives of the people of Afghanistan were improving. Millions of men, women, and children now had the opportunity to go forward with their lives, to pursue education and enjoy freedom.

In fact, making those opportunities come alive was another function of the U.S. military, and many American soldiers were eager to participate in that aspect of the operation. Humanitarian efforts were rewarding and crucially important to the future of the country. "We are here for a short time as a bridge between war and peace," noted army Brigadier General David Kratzer, who commanded the Coalition Joint Civil Military Operations Task Force in 2002. "We leave a footprint for others to follow."[133]

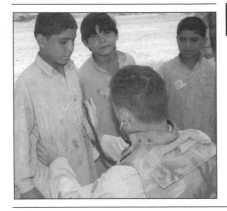

Chapter 6

"This Is My Calling"

To emphasize that the war in Afghanistan was a war on terrorists, not on innocent Afghan citizens, President Bush and other world leaders pledged to provide as much humanitarian aid to the country as possible. Their goal was to illustrate their care and concern, as well as to begin to reverse the devastating effects of two decades of war. Bush defined the extent of America's commitment in a speech at the State Department on October 1, 2001:

> I'm . . . here to announce an initiative to help the Afghan people in a time of crisis and in a time of need. . . . America will contribute an additional $320 million in humanitarian assistance for Afghans for more food, more medicine, to help the innocent people of Afghanistan deal with the coming winter. This is our way of saying that while we firmly and strongly oppose the Taliban regime, we are friends of the Afghan people.[134]

U.S. military men and women strongly supported the president's commitment to help the Afghans. As Americans, they were aware of the many advantages they enjoyed living in one of the richest countries in the world. They also found it difficult to do nothing when women, children, the old, and the infirm were suffering. Thus, with and without government support, they began to reach out to the Afghans in a variety of ways.

Packets from the Sky

The first humanitarian efforts involved men and women in the air rather than on the ground. On October 7, 2001, the U.S. military began a program of providing emergency food supplies to the Afghan people. Hundreds of thousands of Afghan refugees had been driven from their homes by war and drought in recent years, and most faced starvation in the upcoming winter. Food aid was one means of saving their lives, so every night through December, about thirty-seven thousand yellow plastic food packets, known as Humanitarian Daily Rations (HDRs) were dropped from American planes over the country.

Flying at high altitudes to avoid ground fire, crews who delivered the food were more than willing to wear oxygen masks and endure freezing temperatures while the pallets of food were pushed from the back of cargo planes. The packets were about the size and weight of a hardcover book and were designed to flutter to the ground to minimize the risk of injuring someone below. Each had a picture of a person eating from a pouch and a stencil of an American flag on the front. They bore the message: "Food Gift From The People of the United States of America." Each was designed to feed one person for one day. Their contents included vegetarian entrees, peanut butter and jelly, rice protein bars, and other nutritious fare that did not offend Muslim dietary rules. (For instance, Muslims are not allowed to eat pork.)

Food packets known as Humanitarian Daily Rations were dropped from high-flying planes over Afghanistan.

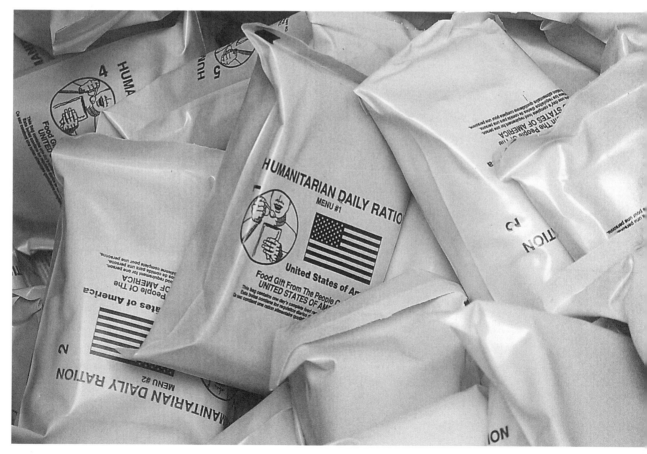

Despite the good intentions behind the drops, some organizations and groups criticized them, pointing out that they were the same color as cluster bombs and thus might confuse children who would pick up the dangerous missiles thinking they were food. Other critics pointed out that the packets could fall into the hands of the Taliban or unscrupulous individuals who might sell them for high prices.

American officials understood the risk and considered a color change for the packets. They believed, however, that given the dire conditions Afghans faced, the drops were worthwhile even if only some were able to benefit. Aircrews who made the deliveries were also convinced that the efforts were invaluable. "Last night was a major milestone, 1 million HDRs delivered, and we will continue to drop HDRs," said Colonel Bob Allardice, a humanitarian airdrop mission commander, on October 31, 2001. "This is symbolic—of our continued effort and commitment to the people of Afghanistan."[135]

Early Efforts

Humanitarian efforts on the ground in Afghanistan were limited while the Taliban was in power, but as soon as American soldiers could move about the country in relative safety, they began helping the population in a variety of ways. At first, their aid was a spontaneous response to a specific

Toys for Guns

Afghanistan is a country where weapons and warfare are common, but as Staff Sergeant Rhonda M. Lawson details in "Army Reserve PSYOP Soldiers Trade Toys for Guns in Kabul," some in the military are doing all they can to change that, starting with the children. The article can be read on the Internet at www.army.mil.

> Army Reserve Staff Sgt. Ed picks up a toy gun that looks strikingly like a silver 9 mm pistol. Out of habit, he puts his finger near the trigger, points the weapon at the floor and cocks it. "These are the ones we want off the street," he says as he places the weapon back on the desk.
>
> The toy was one of about 50 collected Monday morning at the Paktiakot Primary School in Kabul as part of a program to deter children from playing with realistic-looking toy guns. Once a week, Ed and other psychological op-

erations soldiers visit area schools to replace the guns with more harmless toys like cars and plastic soccer balls. The guns are then taken away and destroyed. . . .

The Toys for Guns program, according to Maj. Robert, a civil affairs officer, began as a force protection issue for the military police who patrol Kabul. He explained that as they were doing their patrols, young children would point realistic-looking guns at them. This nearly caused them to retaliate until they realized that the guns were only toys. . . .

Although the children were apprehensive at first about giving up their toys, they soon warmed up to the idea. Now, the children volunteer to bring their guns to school, knowing that they will get something in return. . . . [And] the Toys for Guns program has yielded an unexpected result—increased attendance.

need. For instance, a demining team lent a hand to villagers who reported finding a cache of unexploded weapons. The team removed the danger by detonating the explosives. Special Forces medics treated wounded or sick children whom they encountered as they went out on operations. As word of their compassion spread, the Americans' popularity grew. "People would know that we had the capability for medical care, so they would come up to us and show us every cut, scrape, rash, and old gunshot wound," said one soldier. "They thought we could fix about everything."[136]

Efforts soon became more organized and aimed to help a greater number of people. One of the first tasks to be completed was a safety assessment of the "Friendship Bridge"—an important railway span near the town of Termez, linking Uzbekistan with Afghanistan. The bridge, over which humanitarian supplies could be transported, had been closed since the takeover of Afghanistan by the Taliban. In November 2001, a team of army engineers made the long, dangerous journey to the border, examined the bridge, and declared it structurally sound. In early 2002, after the Uzbek government made necessary repairs, it opened to allow thousands of tons of food and other goods to enter Afghanistan. "We came to the conclusion that the track was serviceable with moderate reconstruction required for the rail ties and the adjacent warehouse facilities,"[137] explained one of the team.

Another humanitarian effort involved providing aid to Afghans who were victims of an earthquake in the mountains of northern Afghanistan on March 26, 2002. After the 6.1 quake devastated the town of Nahrin and other rural parts of Baghlan Province, casualties were calculated to be more than five thousand. Twenty thousand people were left homeless, and the need for aid was apparent.

Traveling by truck or jeep was difficult due to the remoteness of the area, so, as quickly as possible, Special Forces and civil affairs soldiers loaded thousands of pounds of necessary supplies, including cold-weather clothing, water, wheat, MREs, tents, and blankets, into helicopters and flew them to the locale. A large amount of medical supplies was also provided, and medical personnel arrived to help local doctors treat the wounded. "It was a lot of hard work, but we did a good thing. I believe it will help the people of Afghanistan. It was a good effort to get supplies to an area that might not have gotten them if there hadn't been an earthquake,"[138] said Major David Floyd, a medical service officer with the Third Medical Command.

Full-Scale Assistance

After the fall of the Taliban, the U.S. military and forces from other countries who were a part of the war on terror began a full-scale assessment of the damage that needed to be addressed in Afghanistan. Then they got to work. Norwegian demining teams went to work ridding the country of unexploded bombs and land mines. Korean and Jordanian forces provided medical care. From the United States, civil affairs battalions—troops whose job it was to build good relationships with local people while rebuilding the country—paved the way for civilian aid organizations that followed. They opened lines of communication, won the respect of the population, and also took on many construction, accounting, and engineering tasks. Their presence marked the beginning of better times for many Afghans.

Anything that could improve living conditions was tackled, including upgrading water quality, health facilities, communications systems, and infrastructure such as roads and bridges. One civil affairs team helped establish a functioning government in a village in eastern Afghanistan, meeting with local elders and advising them as they created positions such as minister of health, minister of education, and so forth. Communication was difficult because the Americans were not fluent in Pashto, the local dialect, but soldiers tried to adapt. "You try to learn a little bit just to show them you at least want to learn about their culture,"[139] army captain Britton Londo said.

Others helped repair orphanages for some of the thousands of children who had lost their parents during the war decades. Overworked employees in crumbling mud buildings were raising many of these youngsters. At the Rosantun Orphanage nine miles from Bagram, for instance, one hundred children lived in a building with no glass in the windows. At night they slept on a blanket on the floor, in danger of scor-

pion bites, a common problem in the region. Major Bryan Cole, a member of a civil affairs battalion, heard of their situation and helped remedy it. "People with nothing need everything," he observed, and with help from interested individuals at Bagram Air Base and back in the United States, his team was able to provide scarves and slippers, soap, soup, cereal, and toys for the children. "It's a grass-roots effort that has done real well," he notes. "I think we've got the greatest job in Afghanistan. We get outside the wire, meet people, show other soldiers what we're here for."[140]

Back to School

The welfare of children was a top priority with all American soldiers, and rebuilding schools fell in that category. Most schools had been either closed by the Taliban or destroyed by war, so the majority of children were receiving no education at all. Others were being taught in private homes or were meeting outdoors or in schoolhouses with no roofs, no windows, no plumbing, and no electricity.

Civil affairs teams turned their attention to the task, although rather than carry out actual construction projects themselves, they awarded contracts for some of the work to local engineers. Thus, Afghans in need of money could have employment. In the Bamiyan district in central Afghanistan, a team helped rebuild and furnish six schools. Near Kabul, students who used six rusted metal shipping containers as classrooms for nine years finally got a school

Afghan villagers help a U.S. soldier carry school supplies. Military personnel were involved with a number of humanitarian efforts.

building. In Mazār-e Sharīf, the Sultan Razia Girls School, which had been targeted by U.S. forces when Taliban fighters sheltered there, was restored. So was the Parwan Girls School in the Jabul Saraj district. The latter structure was in such disrepair that the students' only water source was a dirty underground stream that flowed through the school. The bathrooms were in a condition that made some of the humanitarian team members half-sick during their assessment. "We specifically wanted to do an all-girls school because we know how they've been suppressed during the Taliban and al-

Qaeda timeframe,"[141] Major John Wiegand, the project leader, explained.

Even when school buildings were functional, soldiers were struck by the lack of supplies. "When we first got here and looked at the conditions, there were no blackboards, no desks,"[142] says Lieutenant Colonel Edward Dorman, speaking of schools near Bagram. To combat the need, engineering battalions constructed desks and benches so students

Girls from Kabul attend class in a school that the U.S. Army helped rebuild.

did not have to sit on the floor. In other areas, they installed woodstoves. Other soldiers provided supplies such as pencils, paper, and books by enlisting the help of caring supporters at home.

The results were rewarding. By the beginning of the 2002–2003 school year, 2 million students were back in class again, many in schoolhouses rebuilt with military aid. "I'd rather help than kill," nineteen-year-old specialist Brian Palmerick said. "And that is what we are doing here."[143]

Not every soldier was confined to construction and supply tasks. Many educated

Afghans had fled the country when the Taliban took power, so a lack of teachers was often more of a problem than a lack of supplies. To help fill the need, some soldiers volunteered their services as teachers on a part-time basis. Two of them were Edward Dorman, who had taught French and German at the U.S. Military Academy at West Point, New York, and Captain Steven Mc-Alpin, an army reservist who was a teacher in civilian life. Both taught conversational

English in Bagram High School, which was short twenty teachers. Local school administrators were delighted to accept their services, and eager Afghan students competed to get into their classes. The experience was extremely rewarding to all. "This is my calling," said McAlpin. "I am first a soldier, always a soldier, but I am also a teacher. I'm having a ball. I love this."[144]

"The American Game"

When it came to "having a ball," a group of American soldiers stationed in the Orgun Valley in eastern Afghanistan found that teaching baseball to Afghan children was not only fun, it helped establish better relationships between themselves and villagers.

"This all started from two kids tossing a ball around,"[145] explained Sergeant William H. Koenig, who was one of the organizers of two baseball teams in the village of Orgun near the Pakistan border. In fact, the wife of Sergeant Jay Smith, a civil affairs engineer, was the one who sent two baseball gloves and a ball in a care package to her husband. Smith gave the articles to two boys he had befriended and taught them to throw and catch.

The project took off from there. Soldiers whittled a bat from a large tent peg. They gave young catchers a bulletproof vest to wear as a chest protector and provided a sandbag for a pitcher's mound. Chalk baselines were drawn using a spent anti-tank shell strapped to a wheeled machine gun carriage.

As games began to be played more regularly, the region's minister of education expressed interest in the project and was shown a videotape of a baseball game (another article in a care package from home). "The

Hopeful Signs

In August 2002, Defense Secretary Donald Rumsfeld and Marine Corps general Peter Pace, vice chairman of the Joint Chiefs of Staff, gave an account of some of the many accomplishments civil affairs teams had made in Afghanistan in the past year. A complete account of the article, "Rumsfeld Praises Civil Affairs' Work in Afghanistan," can be found on the Internet at www.defenselink.mil.

Army civil affairs teams are working in some 10 regions of the country, digging wells, rebuilding schools, bridges and hospitals, [Rumsfeld] pointed out. The Combined Joint Civil-Military Operations Task Force, he said, has completed 58 of 118 scheduled projects in Afghanistan.

"They've rebuilt four regional hospitals and clinics in Kabul, Mazar, Herat and Kunduz," Rumsfeld remarked. They've also put up 38 schools in 10 regions and 75 wells to provide decent drinking water. "And, they've completed reconstruction of the Bagram bridge and the road connecting Bagram to Kabul."

More projects are in the works, he continued, including 10 more medical facilities, 20 more schools, four agricultural projects, two roads, two bridges, and 144 additional wells. . . . "It's still a very dangerous place," Pace cautioned, "but the signs are very good."

minister of education thought it was great," said Sergeant Victor Andersen. "He understood it was the American game, . . . and he thought it would be a great idea for the kids."[146]

A Little League rule book was soon translated into Pashto, and two teams—the Eagles and the Afghans—were formed. Games were not strictly regulation, but the American organizers did insist that anyone playing on a team attend school regularly during the day. As baseball became more popular, more parents turned out to watch,

An Afghan child swings at a pitch as other children and U.S. soldiers cheer. Baseball helped to establish goodwill between American soldiers and Afghan civilians.

An army doctor examines Afghan children who have never had proper medical care.

a sure sign of growing goodwill. "Baseball is here to show them the American way, to show them that we're not here for any other reason than to help out," says Smith. "We're not against [Afghans], we're not against Islam. We can be here together, Afghans and Americans."[147]

Treating Man and Beast

Afghans and American soldiers also worked together when it came to providing better health care for those in need. And the need was acute. Throughout the country, hospitals had suffered from bombing, from power failures, and from an inability to get supplies. Medical personnel had not received training since the 1980s.

Civil affairs teams thus set about hauling away debris from medical facilities. They repaired buildings; restored power; and provided drugs, bandages, equipment, and other necessities. Progress was encouraging. For instance, by May 2002, a quarter of the Karte-Seh Hospital in Kabul was rebuilt and had been given a fresh coat of white paint with blue trim. The civil affairs battalion in charge had overseen the construction of an administrative office, an X-ray room, and a pharmacy.

Medical units concentrated on updating local doctors and nurses on the latest

Egg Yolk and Spit

Sergeant Victor Andersen, a member of the Ninety-Sixth Civil Affairs Battalion spent much of his seven-month term of service providing medical care to the Afghan people. In an article written by Kathleen T. Rhem titled "Special Forces Medic Reaches Out to Afghan People," Andersen provides insight on the level of medical care that was common in Afghanistan prior to 2002 and how American forces were improving that care. Rhem's article can be found on the Internet at www.specialopsmedicine.com.

Andersen said the most common medical treatment before the Americans' arrival was egg yolk and tobacco spit. "They would rub this into any wound," he said. He spoke of a man the team saw who had a dislocated wrist. Here's how local hospital's doctors treated him: "Egg yolk and tobacco spit," Andersen said. "This was their cure for everything."

Andersen said he saw "a hundred years' worth of change" during his stay in terms of medical care available to the local civilian population. "They're so accustomed to no help being available that when someone reaches a condition (of a certain level of seriousness), they expect the person to die," he said. The sergeant noted the Afghans' average life span is 44, "and most don't make it that far."

Andersen said most Afghans seem fairly healthy, but added with some bitterness that's because the ones who aren't healthy die. He said he believes the American soldiers caring for the people and improving the skills of local care providers have begun to change the sense of fatalism held by most Afghan civilians he came to know.

treatments as well. With the new information, health conditions that were formerly considered incurable could be addressed. Hundreds of Afghans who would have suffered and died from diseases such as dysentery and leishmaniasis, a rare skin infection, were cured.

Attending to those who sought treatment inside or outside hospitals was a full-time task. One anesthesiologist, Allen Sturdevant, was deployed to treat Special Forces fighters near the Pakistan border, but spent most of his time attending to villagers who had been shot or had stepped on land mines. A group of American doctors including optometrists, specialists, and general practitioners who visited the village of Kohe Sofi in October 2002 were greeted by more than eight hundred adults and children who sought care. The practitioners spent days treating stomach ailments, headaches, eye problems, and infected wounds. They also handed out deworming medicine, toothbrushes and toothpaste, and brochures on the danger of picking up unexploded bombs. "What we're doing is coming to see ways we can help them. We can help them with vaccines, we can help them with rebuilding hospitals,"[148] said Sergeant Major Louis Matson.

The importance of vaccinating as many citizens as possible against diseases such as diphtheria, tetanus, whooping cough, and polio was illustrated in November 2002. At that time an outbreak of whooping cough occurred in a northeastern district, killing about seventy children and putting another forty thousand at risk. By using U.S. helicopters, medical teams were able to reach the isolated area, which was normally accessible only on horseback. The team vaccinated two thousand people.

While numerous medics focused on providing health care to humans throughout Afghanistan, a small group of veterinarians in one civil affairs battalion decided to make farm animals their focus. The decision was based on practicality. Many families' livelihoods were at least partially based on a donkey to transport goods, on a cow or goat to give milk, or on sheep to provide wool for clothing. Thus owners were eager to keep their animals well, especially after drought and war had decreased cattle and sheep populations by as much as 80 percent since 1998.

The veterinarian team was limited in what it could do on a visit, but it made the best attempt possible. Most treatments had to do with administering vitamin shots, antibiotics, or deworming medicines. Wounds and other conditions that would impact the animals' health were also given attention. The aid might be only short-term, but it was better than nothing. "Will doing these sporadic [visits], medical or veterinary, save this country?" asks veterinarian Lieutenant Colonel Robert Sindlar. "No. That's something that will only happen at a level far above where we operate. But if this helps out just temporarily, if it could save a cow, or just make an animal live longer. That's a positive thing."[149]

New Army, New Outlook

In a category far different from health care but just as important to Afghanistan's future, in April 2002 American troops began training a new national army that would eventually take over the defense of the new government and the nation. Classes, which began with the basics and progressed to more complex skills, were led by about one hundred and fifty U.S. Army Special Forces who allotted about ten weeks to train each group of recruits. "The trainees undergo four weeks of individual movement techniques and basic rifle marksmanship, two weeks heavy weapons and two weeks collective training including a final field and live-fire exercise,"[150] explained one trainer known only as Dan.

The need for a national army was recognized when Hamid Karzai's transitional national government took over the country in December 2001. Tribal and regional loyalties played enormous roles in Northern Alliance militias. Most soldiers were untrained, undisciplined, and devoted only to a local warlord from their part of the country. "Most of these soldiers already knew each other before they got here," said Dan. "This was a problem at the beginning because many of them are from different tribes and their initial instinct was to quarrel."[151]

In order to ensure loyalty to the new government, a shift in philosophy was necessary. The American soldiers set out to instill it. They emphasized that the new army would be under the command of the Afghan Ministry of Defense, centered in the capital of Kabul. Ethnic backgrounds were de-emphasized, and a feeling of teamwork and mutual reliance among the trainees was established. Instructors pushed rigorous training and tried to infuse a sense of pride in belonging to the new army. To reinforce that, they provided new uniforms and a unique identification patch, designed specifically for graduates.

Although the army project would require time and patience before it was complete, in September 2002, the first class graduated. The members' new outlook was encouraging. Many had made friends with lifelong enemies. All were focused on the work ahead. "We are all one people now with one common goal—to defend Afghanistan," said one graduate. "We are very happy to have

Afghan soldiers line up to receive new uniforms and equipment before training with U.S. Army Special Forces.

formed an army where there are no tribes or ethnicities to set us apart."[152]

The world saw the new army as just one of the essentials if Afghanistan were to remain an independent, terrorist-free nation. "In the end, we've got to train Afghan forces to deal with . . . pockets [of al-Qaeda and the Taliban] themselves,"[153] says Joint Chiefs of Staff chairman General Richard Myers. Another essential was the gradual removal of foreign (i.e., U.S.) troops. No one, least of all the United States, wanted to become permanent peacekeepers in the region.

Even with the help of the Afghan people, however, at the end of a year there remained much work for American forces to do. Osama bin Laden was wily and had plenty of funds to carry out his terrorist acts. He had the support of other extremist organizations and anti-Western governments around the world. In addition, remnants of the Taliban remained in Afghanistan, capable of attempting another takeover. As a whole, the outlook at times seemed bleak. Experts such as Dr. Paul Cornish of London's Centre for Defense Studies were more philosophical.

> You have to look at what was achieved within a very short time, and it was quite a remarkable achievement. But I don't think that anybody was seriously expecting that the whole thing could have been wound up and bagged up in a very short time. . . . There was always a sense that this was going to take quite a while, given the country and the embedded (nature) of various factions in Afghanistan.[154]

Chapter 7

Beyond Afghanistan

T he second year of war in Afghanistan began very differently from the first. The Taliban government had been ousted. Al-Qaeda could no longer operate with impunity within the country. A new, moderate government was in place. The Afghan people could work, shop, dress, and educate their children as they pleased.

On the other hand, the hunt for Taliban and al-Qaeda operatives continued. Combat deaths still occurred. The American presence in Afghanistan was still very necessary if the enemy—or another just like him—was not to return and breed terror. Some observers were beginning to wonder if the conflict could ever be brought to an end, or if U.S. troops were going to be in the country indefinitely.

Homecoming

Thousands of American soldiers seemed destined to remain in Afghanistan far into the future. In 2002, numbers actually climbed from four thousand in January to more than seven thousand in October. But for many men and women, participation in the conflict was over. They had served six or more months in combat and had thus earned the right to return to the United States and to their families.

After the long trip halfway around the world, returning soldiers were transported back to locales from which they had taken off the year before. These were often bases such as Fort Bragg, North Carolina, and Fort Lewis, Washington, as well as home ports such as San Diego, California, and Pearl Harbor, Hawaii. No matter where they landed, all were extremely excited to be home and to see familiar landmarks. Most anticipated a happy homecoming. Spouses and children were there to meet the soldiers when they landed, carrying hand-lettered signs with messages that read "I Love You" and "Welcome Home from the 'Stan."

Meetings were usually warm and sentimental. Babies cried. Small children looked self-conscious when they were hugged by a virtual stranger named "Daddy." Flags waved and balloons floated overhead. Wives' clubs handed out red roses to the returnees, and returnees handed sweethearts and wives bouquets of roses in return. "It was just us and our families. It was great," Sergeant Michael Peterson said of his homecoming in November 2002. "I went through the ticker tape stuff after the Gulf War. You don't need that. You just need your family." [155]

Unsettled Memories

Despite the joy of the reunions, however, some men and women—particularly those who had done hard fighting in the campaign—carried with them memories of fear, death, and dying that did not easily fade. "It'll always be there," said twenty-three-year-old Andrew Spurlock, referring to the fact that

A returning U.S. airman embraces his five-month-old daughter for the first time.

he killed an enemy fighter he found hiding in a cave, "but I didn't change any."[156]

The lingering memories of war and the devastation of Afghanistan sometimes made adjusting to life at home extremely difficult. Noisy children, expectations of friends and family, and the pressure of the daily routine could be hard to cope with after months away. A few men and women became depressed and withdrew from relationships. Preexistent marital difficulties sometimes worsened.

Such difficulties may have been a contributing factor in several murder/suicide incidents that took place at Fort Bragg, North Carolina, in June and July of 2002. At that time, four soldiers stationed at the fort killed their wives and then, in two instances, killed themselves. All the men were special operations servicemen, and three had recently returned from the war.

No concrete evidence pointed to war as being the primary cause of the tragedies, but the connection could not be ignored. The fact that special operations men were trained to be strong and self-reliant meant that they were often unwilling to seek help for emotional problems that might arise as a result of combat. Colonel David Hackworth, a veteran of three wars, observed, "They perform secretive missions that are high stress, and then they come home and can't talk about it with their wives. When you add the violence of fighting, returning home under these circumstances can be a problem."[157]

The Mission Gets Complicated

For those soldiers who remained in Afghanistan after mid-2002, combat duty was stressful and liable to produce anger and frustration. For some, the situation seemed similar to the Vietnam War in the 1960s, when ill-defined objectives made the conflict impossible to win.

Instead of engaging in full-scale battles against the Taliban army, troops became involved in seemingly endless hunts for hard-to-find Taliban and al-Qaeda operatives. They were harassed almost daily by rocket fire and hit-and-run attacks, but rarely saw who was attacking them. Their assignments were complicated by language barriers and by the fact that many Afghans had become increasingly resentful of having Americans in their country and therefore were uncooperative or even belligerent.

Attempts to track down terrorists were also hampered by inaccurate or misleading information provided by locals. For instance, one Special Forces team that entered Chaghcharan, a remote village in eastern Afghanistan, was told by the police chief that one thousand Taliban were hiding in a nearby valley, waiting to ambush the unit when it came looking for them. "They will let you in, then close off your escape and kill you all,"[158] the chief opined, suggesting that the Americans call in bombers to clean out the region before going in.

Other villagers told a different story, however. They claimed that the Taliban fighters had left the valley long before, and that only innocent civilians lived there now. Un-

Afghan president Hamid Karzai (seated, right) has faced many difficulties since taking office.

sure what to expect, the unit made careful preparations and went in, only to discover that the Taliban were indeed gone. Later they learned that the chief had pushed to have the valley bombed because some of his own personal enemies lived there. He had simply wanted a private revenge.

More Complications

Such deviousness proved to be a hindrance. So was the ability of the enemy to pass as an ordinary citizen or even a loyal supporter of the government, and in such a way to position himself to strike. One example of this

was the assassination attempt on President Hamid Karzai in September 2002. Karzai had gone to Kandahar to celebrate his nephew's wedding and was visiting the governor's palace, when a uniformed man opened fire upon him and his entourage. Karzai was protected by his bodyguards, who shot and killed the attacker. The man proved to be a Taliban supporter who had successfully gotten a job as a palace guard a few weeks earlier.

The Next Chapter

In his State of the Union address on January 28, 2003, President George W. Bush defined his next target in the war against terrorism—dictator Saddam Hussein's repressive and dangerous Iraqi regime. More excerpts from Bush's address can be accessed on the Internet at www.whitehouse.gov.

> Today, the gravest danger in the war on terror, the gravest danger facing America and the world, is outlaw regimes that seek and possess nuclear, chemical, and biological weapons. These regimes could use such weapons for blackmail, terror, and mass murder. They could also give or sell those weapons to terrorist allies, who would use them without the least hesitation.
>
> This threat is new; America's duty is familiar. . . .
>
> The world has waited 12 years for Iraq to disarm. America will not accept a serious and mounting threat to our country, and our friends and our allies. The United States will ask the U.N. Security Council to convene on February the 5th to consider the facts of Iraq's ongoing defiance of the world. Secretary of State [Colin] Powell will present information and intelligence about Iraq's . . . illegal weapons programs, its attempt to hide those weapons from inspectors, and its links to terrorist groups.

> We will consult. But let there be no misunderstanding: If Saddam Hussein does not fully disarm, for the safety of our people and for the peace of the world, we will lead a coalition to disarm him.

Iraq's Saddam Hussein became the second target in the United States's war on terrorism.

Changing loyalties and infighting between rival Afghan commanders also complicated the American mission. Most were cooperative and trustworthy only when it served their personal interests. As a result, it was dangerous to rely on them too completely. One such individual was Hajji Saifullah who had been a high-ranking Taliban commander before throwing his support to the United States. Another was Rashid Dostum, who put fighting with a ri-val before service to the national government.

Gulbuddin Hekmatyar, a former prime minister of Afghanistan, was perhaps one of the most powerful and dangerous. Hekmatyar had once been a U.S. ally, but over time his loyalties shifted. By 2003, he had allied himself with the Taliban and al-Qaeda and attacked a Special Forces unit in eastern Afghanistan. "[Hekmatyar's force is] without a doubt the largest concentration of enemy forces that we've come across since Operation Anaconda,"[159] Colonel Roger King stated, referring to the fact that Hekmatyar's own militia had joined forces with Taliban fighters who had been hiding in the mountains.

Standing Ready

With so many obstacles to success, a quick and definitive victory in the war in Afghanistan seems unlikely. Especially troubling to the military were reports in early 2003 showing that al-Qaeda and Taliban forces were again seeking to garner support among Afghans in order to rebuild their base of operations in Afghanistan.

Added to that is the frustration over America's inability to capture the primary target in the war, Osama bin Laden. All know that the danger will not end with his capture. Other members of al-Qaeda are as qualified to lead the terrorist cause as he has been. Nevertheless, he stands as the definitive enemy, and his capture will be the ultimate symbol of success. "It's like looking for a needle in a haystack . . . ," Secretary of Defense Donald Rumsfeld said in late 2001.

"But we certainly intend to find him, and we're doing everything humanly possible to do that."[160]

Until that happens, all men and women of the military remain ready to fight in Afghanistan or wherever else danger may threaten. Incidents of terrorism lead many to speculate that other wars in the near future are likely and could take place in the Philippines, Yemen, Pakistan, or other countries where terrorists lurk. In late 2002, President Bush indicated that Saddam Hussein's menacing regime in Iraq would be his next focus in the military campaign, and military leaders began combat operations there in March 2003.

No matter what the locale, American soldiers understand their purpose—to defend, protect, and serve as long as they are needed. As Rumsfeld notes, "The task will be a long one, and it's not the kind of thing where there's a set . . . battle and you either win it or lose it. We're going to have to stay at the terrorists wherever they are, find them and root them out. But we'll win it, let there be no doubt. It started in Afghanistan, but it won't end there."[161]

✫ Notes ✫

Introduction: "A Certain Force in an Uncertain World"

1. Quoted in Melissa Phillips, "Tech. Sgt. Keith Winchell," Defend America, September 18, 2002. www.defendamerica.mil.

2. Quoted in Rudi Williams, "Reflections on Sept. 11, a Day of Terror," Defense Link, September 11, 2002. www.defenselink.mil.

3. Quoted in Phillips, "Tech. Sgt. Keith Winchell."

4. Quoted in Barton Gelman, "Clinton's War on Terror," *Washington Post,* December 19, 2001. www.washingtonpost.com.

5. Quoted in Phillips, "Tech. Sgt. Keith Winchell."

6. Quoted in *Frontline,* "Interview: U.S. Army Captain Jason Amerine," 2002. www.pbs.org.

7. J.A. Scordo, "Current Status," 26th Marine Expeditionary Unit, April 24, 2001. www.26meu.usmc.mil.

8. Quoted in April Middleton, "Soldier's Personal, Work Life Altered," *Kansas State Collegian,* September 11, 2002. www.kstatecollegian.com.

Chapter 1: War in a Far-Off Land

9. Philip Cheng and Laurie McBean, "Fly-through Data Generation of Afghanistan," *Earth Observation Magazine,* January 2002. www.eomonline.com.

10. Rina Amiri, "Comprehending the Quagmire," *Sojourner,* November 2001. www.sojourner.org.

11. Quoted in Robert McMahon, "UN: Security Council Condemns Taliban for Afghan Instability," *Radio Free Europe,* April 8, 2000. www.rferl.org.

12. *MSNBC News,* "Massoud's Last Words," September 20, 2001. www.msnbc.com.

13. Osama bin Laden, "Jihad Against Jews and Crusaders," Jihad Unspun, February 23, 1998. www.jihadunspun.net.

14. Jim Kolbe, "Speech Before US Navy League and USS TUCSON 770 Club," United States Representative Jim Kolbe's Website, October 20, 2000. www.house.gov.

15. Quoted in Barbara Starr, "As Pentagon Burned, Plans for War Took Shape," *CNN,* September 6, 2002. www.cnn.com.

16. Quoted in Kathleen T. Rhem, "Franks: A Leader Sure of His Mission and His Troops," Defense Link, January 5, 2002. www.defenselink.mil.

17. Quoted in Rhem, "Franks: A Leader Sure of His Mission and His Troops."

18. Quoted in Nic Robertson and Kelly Wallace, "U.S. Rejects Taliban Offer to

Try Bin Laden," *CNN*, October 7, 2001. www.cnn.com.

19. Quoted in David Levinsky, "First Active-duty Airmen Move Out from McGuire," *Burlington County Times,* September 21, 2001. www.phillyburbs.com.

20. Quoted in James C. McKinley Jr., "At Fort Drum, Family and Nuptial Worries," *New York Times,* September 22, 2001, p. B10.

Chapter 2: Getting Ready to Go

21. Quoted in James Dao, "Eerie Quiet as 'Screaming Eagles' Await Battle Orders," *New York Times,* September 24, 2001, p. A1.

22. Quoted in Susan H. Greenberg, "Get Out of My Way," *MSNBC News,* October 29, 2001. www.msnbc.com.

23. Quoted in Amanda Currier, "Airman Basic Amy Ting," Defend America, 2003. www.defendamerica.mil.

24. Quoted in U.S. Army, "Recruit Profile: Basic Training," 2003. www.goarmy.com.

25. Quoted in Brian Coughlin, *Basic Training,* A&E Television Networks, 2002.

26. Quoted in Jim Garamone, "Rite of Passage," Defense Link, 2002. www.defenselink.mil.

27. Patrick D. McGowan, "Preface," Outside the Wire, no date. http://outsidethewire.net.

28. Quoted in U.S. Army, "Soldier Profiles," 2003. www.goarmy.com.

29. Quoted in Rowan Scarborough, "'Special Ops' Gets OK to Initiate Its Own Missions," *Washington Times,* January 8, 2003. www.washtimes.com.

30. Quoted in Linda D. Kozaryn, "Army Reserve Duty Has 'Changed Forever,'" Defense Link, January 22, 2002. www.defenselink.mil.

31. Quoted in Beena Maharaj, "Portrait of a Citizen Airman," *The Officer,* May 2002, p. 17.

32. Quoted in Brian Perry, "It's a Beautiful Day: Arrival in Afghanistan," *The Officer,* June 2002, p. 16.

33. Quoted in Kozaryn, "Army Reserve Duty Has 'Changed Forever.'"

34. Quoted in Steve Olafson, "Reservists, Troops Getting Affairs in Order," *Houston Chronicle,* September 15, 2001. www.chron.com.

35. Quoted in Olafson, "Reservists, Troops Getting Affairs in Order."

36. Quoted in Dao, "Eerie Quiet as 'Screaming Eagles' Await Battle Orders," p. A1.

37. Quoted in Karin Schmidt, "Knight's Tale: A Call to Action for Nurse Reservist," *Nurse Week,* November 11, 2001. www.nurseweek.com.

38. Quoted in Jon Ostendorff, "Families Eagerly Await 211th's Return," *Asheville Citizen-Times,* September 10, 2002. http://cgi.citizen-times.com.

39. Quoted in Olafson, "Reservists, Troops Getting Affairs in Order."

40. Quoted in Olafson, "Reservists, Troops Getting Affairs in Order."

41. Quoted in *Fox News,* "Military Couples Rush to Get Married," September 25, 2001. www.foxnews.com.

42. Quoted in Jennifer Dyer Cornelisson, "Just the Two of Us, Married Without Children," LIFElines Services Network, 2003. www.lifelines2000.org.

43. Quoted in J.A. Scordo, "Current Status."

44. Quoted in *Warships International Fleet Review,* "USS Kitty Hawk Carries the War to the Terrorist," March 2003. www.warshipsifr.com.

45. Quoted in J.A. Scordo, "Current Status."

46. Quoted in 26th MEU, "Preparing to Go," November 28, 2001. http://192.156.19.109/marinelink/mcn2000.nsf.

47. The White House, "President: 'We're Making Progress,'" October 1, 2001. www.whitehouse.gov.

Chapter 3: Living in "the 'Stan"

48. Quoted in *CNN,* "U.S. Special Operations Troops in Commando Raid," October 22, 2001. www.cnn.com.

49. Quoted in Drew Brown, "Land Mines Would Pose Major Threat to U.S. Troops in Afghanistan, Experts Say," Knight-Ridder/Tribune News Service, October 12, 2001. p. K7265.

50. Quoted in *Frontline,* "Interview: U.S. Special Forces ODA 595," 2002. www.pbs.org.

51. Quoted in *Frontline,* "Interview: U.S. Special Forces ODA 595."

52. Quoted in *Frontline,* "Interview: U.S. Special Forces ODA 595."

53. Quoted in *Frontline,* "Interview: U.S. Special Forces ODA 595."

54. Quoted in *Frontline,* "Interview: U.S. Special Forces ODA 595."

55. Quoted in Joseph R. Chenelly, "Marines Land, Seize Desert Strip," Marine Corps Website, November 25, 2001. www.15meu.usmc.mil.

56. Quoted in Robert Hayes, "Army Medic Supports U.S. Forces in Afghanistan," Hometown Link, 2002. http://hn.afnews.af.mil.

57. Quoted in Cassie Tarpley, "Inside Camp Rhino," *Shelby Star,* April 8, 2002. www.shelbystar.com.

58. Quoted in Thomas Michael Corcoran, "Soviet-era Gear Makes Life Easier for Servicemembers at Kandahar Airport," Marine Corps Website, December 31, 2001. www.usmc.mil.

59. Quoted in Stephan McGuire, "From Queens to Kandahar and Back: Answering the Call to Fight Terrorism," *Southeast Queens Press,* September 11, 2002. www.queenspress.com.

60. Quoted in Louis A. Arana-Barradas, "Bagram Troops Live in Austere Conditions," Air Force Link, March 5, 2002. www.af.mil.

61. Quoted in *Jefferson City News Tribune,* "Marines Patrol Base, Review Security After Firefight During First Prisoner Transfer," January 11, 2002. http://newstribune.com.

62. Quoted in Arana-Barradas, "Bagram Troops Live in Austere Conditions."

63. Quoted in Slobodan Lekic, "USS *Constellation* Crew Has Christmas a Day Early," *News Tribune,* December 25, 2002, p. A4.

61. Quoted in Tamara Lush, "Heaven in Time of War: 6700 Ribeyes," *St. Petersburg Times,* July 2, 2002. www.sptimes.com.

65. Quoted in Third Age, Inc., "Preventing Disease Is Tough in Afghanistan," 2003. www.thirdage.com.

66. Quoted in Soldiers for the Truth Foundation, "Troops Latest Afghan Peril: Altitude," 2002. www.sftt.org.

67. Quoted in Beth Miller, "For U.S. Troops, Daily Life Is Filled with Dangers," *News Journal,* April 17, 2002. www.delawareonline.com.

68. Quoted in Rick Reilly, "One Man's Super Bowl," *Sports Illustrated,* October 22, 2001, p. 106.

69. Quoted in Allen Pizzey, "Troops Take a Break in Afghanistan," *CBS News,* December 25, 2002. www.cbsnews.com.

70. Quoted in *Sydney Morning Herald,* "Blue Christmas for Foreign Troops in Afghanistan," December 25, 2002. www.smh.com.au.

71. Quoted in *USA Today,* "U.S. Forces Using the Net to Contact Home," May 7, 2002. www.usatoday.com.

72. Quoted in Rex McCarty, "Shoemaker Elementary Provides Gift Items to American Soldiers," *Scott County Virginia Star,* 2002. www.virginiastar.net.

73. Quoted in Army Link News, "Troops in Afghanistan Mark Holiday with Turkey, Minefield Marathon," December 3, 2002. www.dtic.mil.

74. Martin Savidge, "A-Scrounging We Will Go," *CNN,* February 4, 2002. www.cnn.com.

75. Quoted in David Zucchino, "Chasing Phantoms Across Afghanistan," *Los Angeles Times,* December 29, 2002, p. A1.

Chapter 4: In Pursuit of bin Laden

76. The White House, "Address to a Joint Session of Congress and the American People," September 20, 2001. www.whitehouse.gov.

77. Quoted in Seymour M. Hersh, "Escape and Evasion," *New Yorker,* November 12, 2001. www.newyorker.com.

78. Quoted in Andrew England, "Planes, Pilots and Carrier Crew Pushed to the Limit in Afghanistan Campaign," South Coast Today.com, December 15, 2001. www.s-t.com.

79. Quoted in Mark Oliva and Wayne Specht, "Fully Loaded, AC-130 Spectre Gunship Is Like an Airborne Tank," CheckPoint, October 21, 2001. www.checkpoint-online.ch.

80. Quoted in Reilly, "One Man's Super Bowl," p. 106.

81. Quoted in Chance Babin, "Bombs Away," *Citizen Airman,* June 2002. www.afrc.af.mil.

82. Quoted in Martin Bentham and Adam Lusher, "I Was Smiling: I Had Dropped My Bombs. They Hit,'" *Spectator,* October 21, 2001. www.telegraph.co.uk.

83. Quoted in Bentham and Lusher, "'I Was Smiling: I Had Dropped My Bombs. They Hit.'"

84. Quoted in Babin, "Bombs Away."

85. Quoted in Jeffrey Kofman, "The Tip of the Sword," *ABC News*, October 12, 2001. http://abcnews.go.com.

86. Quoted in Gordon T. Lee, "Hard-Shelled, SOF-Centered: The Synergy of Might and Mind," *Rand Review*, Summer 2002. www.rand.org.

87. Quoted in Lee, "Hard-Shelled, SOF-Centered: The Synergy of Might and Mind."

88. Quoted in *Frontline*, "Interview: U.S. Special Forces ODA 595."

89. Quoted in *Frontline*, "Interview: U.S. Special Forces ODA 595."

90. Quoted in *Frontline*, "Interview: U.S. Special Forces ODA 595."

91. Quoted in *Frontline*, "Interview: U.S. Army Captain Jason Amerine."

92. Quoted in *Frontline*, "The Fall of Kandahar," 2002. www.pbs.org.

93. Quoted in Scott Johnson, "A Sleepless Night in the Cold," *Newsweek*, March 18, 2002, p. 28.

94. Quoted in Gregg Zoroya, "Commandos Fight Abroad Also a Hit at Home," *USA Today*, February 5, 2002. www.usatoday.com.

95. Quoted in Michelle Boorstein, "Soldiers Find Documents in Abandoned Al-Qaida Caves, Then Destroy the Hideouts in Operation Mountain Lion," Efreedom News.com, April 6, 2002. www.efreedomnews.com.

96. Quoted in Andrew Morse, James Blue III, and Marni Harriman, "First Wave: The Soldiers' Story," *ABC News*, March 22, 2002. http://abcnews.go.com.

97. Quoted in Morse, Blue, and Harriman, "First Wave: The Soldiers' Story."

98. Quoted in *ABC News*, "Anaconda Wraps Up," March 18, 2002. http://abcnews.go.com.

99. Quoted in Robert Young Pelton, "The Legend of Heavy D & the Boys," *National Geographic Adventure*, March 2002, p. 66.

100. Quoted in *Frontline*, "Friendly Fire," 2002. www.pbs.org.

101. Quoted in Craig Gordon, "Killed by Friendly Fire," *Newsday*, December 6, 2001. www.globalsecurity.org.

102. Quoted in Michael Ware, "On the Mop-Up Patrol," *Time*, March 25, 2002, p. 45.

103. Quoted in Ware, "On the Mop-Up Patrol," p. 44.

104. Quoted in *CBS News*, "U.S. Troops Hurt in Ambush Flown Out," July 29, 2002. www.cbsnews.com.

105. Quoted in Noelle Phillips, "In the Rear with the Gear," *Savannah Morning News*, April 21, 2002. www.savannahnow.com.

Chapter 5: Behind the Scenes

106. Quoted in Phillips, "In the Rear with the Gear."

107. Quoted in Judith Williams, "Psychologist Gets Underway Aboard Kitty Hawk," *Navy and Marine Corps Medical News*, October 17, 1996. www.chinfo.navy.mil.

108. Quoted in Reeba Critser, "Female MPs Join Infantry on Front Lines," Army Link News, October 30, 2002. www.dtic.mil.

109. Quoted in Gerald M. Carbone, "War on Terrorism—Bomb Squad," *Providence Journal,* October 28, 2001. http://multimedia.belointeractive.com.

110. Quoted in Babin, "Bombs Away."

111. Quoted in Chris King, "Reservists Provide Experience for Expeditionary Squadron," *Officer,* June 2002, p. 17.

112. Quoted in King, "Reservists Provide Experience for Expeditionary Squadron."

113. Quoted in Louis A. Arana-Barradas, "Airmen Making Calm Out of Chaos in Afghanistan," Air Force Link, March 4, 2002. www.af.mil.

114. Quoted in Arana-Barradas, "Airmen Making Calm Out of Chaos in Afghanistan."

115. Quoted in Douglas Ritter, "Aerial Refueling," *Code One Magazine,* January 1993. www.codeonemagazine.com.

116. Quoted in Chuck Goudie, "I-Team Exclusive: Chicagoans at the Front," *ABC News,* October 17, 2001. http://abclocal.go.com.

117. Quoted in Military Woman Home Page, "Inflight Refueler Boom Operator," June 14, 2000. www.militarywoman.org.

118. Quoted in Ritter, "Aerial Refueling."

119. Quoted in Randy Britton, "Reserve Seabees Pave Way for Enduring Freedom in Afghanistan," *Naval Reservist News,* May 2002. www.navres.navy.mil.

120. Quoted in Britton, "Reserve Seabees Pave Way for Enduring Freedom in Afghanistan."

121. Quoted in Vic Harris, "Soldiers Find Water in Drought-Stricken Afghanistan," dcmilitary.com, January 25, 2002. www.dcmilitary.com.

122. Quoted in Vic Harris, "Soldiers Find Water in Drought-Stricken Afghanistan."

123. Quoted in Mike Vernon, "Daily Life in Kandahar," *CBC News,* May 20, 2002. http://cbc.ca.

124. Quoted in Phillips, "In the Rear with the Gear."

125. Quoted in Joseph Giordono, "Deminers Slowly Clear Bagram Base," *European-Pacific Stars and Stripes,* June 30, 2002. www.roncoconsulting.com.

126. Quoted in Giordono, "Deminers Slowly Clear Bagram Base."

127. Quoted in Janet Boivin, "Men Make Their Mark in Military Nursing," *Nursing Spectrum,* November 1, 2002. http://community.nursingspectrum.com.

128. Quoted in Stephen Kaufman, "Military Doctors Attend to Detainee Maladies at Camp X-Ray," U.S. Department of State, February 28, 2002. http://usinfo.state.gov.

129. Quoted in Stephen Kaufman, "Detainees, Guards Interact with Care at Camp X-Ray," U.S. Department of State, February 27, 2002. http://usinfo.state.gov.

130. Quoted in Bob Haskell, "Guarding Terrorists," National Guard Association of the United States, February 2002. www.ngaus.org.

131. Quoted in Haskell, "Guarding Terrorists."

132. Quoted in Haskell, "Guarding Terrorists."

133. Quoted in Susan B. Glasser, "Soldiers in Civilian Clothing," Associated Press, March 28, 2002. www.miraserve.com.

Chapter 6: "This Is My Calling"

134. The White House, "President Directs Humanitarian Aid to Afghanistan," October 4, 2001. www.whitehouse.gov.

135. Quoted in Joe Bela, "AF Makes 1 Millionth Food Drop to Afghanistan," Air Force Link, October 31, 2001. www.af.mil.

136. Quoted in Kathleen T. Rhem, "SF Soldier Works with Army Reserve Medics," United States Army Reserve, 2002. www.army.mil.

137. Quoted in Army Link News, "Soldiers Helping Assess Afghan Infrastructure," January 11, 2002. www.dtic.mil.

138. Quoted in Holly Plata, "Soldiers Bring Relief After Afghan Earthquake," Army Link News, April 9, 2002. www.dtic.mil.

139. Quoted in Kathleen T. Rhem, "Civil Affairs Soldiers Assist Afghan Students, Leaders," Defense Link, October 18, 2002. www.defenselink.mil.

140. Quoted in *Milwaukee Journal Sentinel*, "U.S. Soldiers Visit Afghan Orphans," July 28, 2002. www.jsonline.com.

141. Quoted in Rhonda M. Lawson, "Army Helps Open Three Afghan Schools," Army Link News, September 17, 2002. www.dtic.mil.

142. Quoted in Dave Marck, "Soldiers Teach in Afghan School," Army Link News, April 25, 2002. www.dtic.mil.

143. Quoted in Bryan Mitchell, "District Soldier Working to Make Life Better," U.S. Army Corps of Engineers, 2003. www.orn.usace.army.mil.

144. Quoted in Marck, "Soldiers Teach in Afghan School."

145. Quoted in LaTorry Sidney, "Baseball Comes to Afghanistan," United States Central Command, August 24, 2002. www.centcom.mil.

146. Quoted in Kathleen T. Rhem, "Soldiers Bring America's Pastime to Afghan Children," Defense Link, October 21, 2002. www.defenselink.mil.

147. Quoted in David Buchbinder, "U.S. Troops Bring Little League to Afghanistan," *Christian Science Monitor*, August 19, 2002. www.csmonitor.com.

148. Quoted in Matt Mientka, "Army Medics Aid Afghanistan," *U.S. Medicine*, October 2002. www.usmedicine.com.

149. Quoted in Mike Eckel, "U.S. Veterinarians Are Working in Afghanistan," Associated Press, December 5, 2002. http://story.news.yahoo.com.

150. Quoted in Christina Carde, "Afghan Army Graduates Fifth Battalion," Army Link News, January 9, 2003. www.dtic.mil.

151. Quoted in Carde, "Afghan Army Graduates Fifth Battalion."

152. Quoted in Carde, "Afghan Army Graduates Fifth Battalion."

153. Quoted in Ann Scott Tyson, "US Finds Building Afghan Army Isn't Easy,"

Christian Science Monitor, March 13, 2002. www.csmonitor.com.

154. Quoted in Kathleen Knox, "Afghanistan: Renewed Fighting Raises Question of U.S. 'Exit Strategy,'" *Radio Free Europe,* March 4, 2002. www.rferl.org.

Chapter 7: Beyond Afghanistan

155. Quoted in Ron Kampeas, "Troops Adjust to Return Home," TeamCares, Inc., November 29, 2002. www.teamcares.org.

156. Quoted in Michelle Boorstein, "American Soldiers Return from Afghanistan," *Corpus Christi Caller-Times,* April 4, 2002. www.caller.com.

157. Quoted in Steve Osunsami, "Under Pressure," *ABC News,* July 29, 2002. http://abcnews.go.com.

158. Quoted in Zucchino, "Chasing Phantoms Across Afghanistan," p. A1.

159. Quoted in *CBS News,* "Allied Troops Battle Afghan Rebels," January 28, 2003. www.cbsnews.com.

160. Quoted in Kathleen T. Rhem, "Rumsfeld Believes U.S. Can Get Bin Laden," Defense Link, October 25, 2001. www.defenselink.mil.

161. Quoted in Johnny Rhea, "Rumsfeld: War on Terrorism Not 'Easy, Quick Fix,'" Air Force Link, June 11, 2002. www.af.mil.

★ Glossary ★

Airborne: Those military forces who are paratroopers.

al-Qaeda: International terrorist organization, composed of conservative Muslims and led by Osama bin Laden.

bunker busting bomb: Five-thousand-pound bomb that can penetrate up to twenty-two feet of earth and concrete before exploding.

Central Command (CENTCOM): One of nine unified combatant commands that control U.S. combat forces around the world. Includes all army, navy, air force, and marine units that operate in an area encompassing twenty-five nations and stretching from northern Africa and the Persian Gulf to southwest Asia.

cluster bombs: Small explosive bomblets that are delivered to their targets in larger canisters or shells.

covert: Carried out in secret.

daisy cutter bomb: The largest conventional bomb in the world, first used in Vietnam to clear ground for helicopters to land.

deploy: To place according to a plan.

guerrillas: A small force of irregular soldiers who make surprise raids on an enemy army.

hypothermia: A subnormal body temperature.

Military Occupational Specialty (MOS): Job assignment given to military men and women after basic training. Some MOSs are health care specialist, satellite-systems communications operator, and construction engineering supervisor.

mujahideen: "Holy warriors;" committed Muslims who fought the Soviets in Afghanistan in the 1980s.

ordnance: Military weapons and equipment.

smart bomb: High-technology bomb that is guided to its target by satellite positioning systems.

sortie: One mission or attack by a single plane.

Taliban: Fundamentalist Muslims who seized political power in Afghanistan in 1996.

★ For Further Reading ★

George W. Bush, *A Charge to Keep*. New York: Morrow, 1999. First-person account of Bush's life prior to becoming president.

D.J. Herda, *The Afghan Rebels: The War in Afghanistan*. New York: Franklin Watts, 1990. History of tribal and religious issues in the 1980s Soviet-Afghan War.

Elaine Landau, *Osama bin Laden: A War Against the West*. Brookfield, CT: Twenty-First Century Books, 2002. Biography of the terrorist leader.

Latifa, et. al., *My Forbidden Face: Growing Up Under the Taliban*. New York: Hyperion, 2001. Account of the life of a young Afghan girl growing up under Taliban rule.

☆ Works Consulted ☆

Books

Michael Griffin, *Reaping the Whirlwind: The Taliban Movement in Afghanistan*. London: Pluto Press, 2001. Eyewitness account of conflict in Afghanistan prior to the United States' entrance. Explores the Taliban's connections with Osama bin Laden.

Documentaries

Brian Coughlin, *Basic Training*, A&E Television Networks, 2002. Series documenting the progress made by six recruits going through basic training in the army.

Periodicals

Drew Brown, "Land Mines Would Pose Major Threat to U.S. Troops in Afghanistan, Experts Say," Knight-Ridder/Tribune News Service, October 12, 2001.

James Dao, "Eerie Quiet as 'Screaming Eagles' Await Battle Orders," *New York Times*, September 24, 2001.

John Gittelsohn, "Soldier Recounts Fateful Operation Anaconda Battle," Knight-Ridder/Tribune News Service, April 3, 2002.

Saul Ingle, "'It's My Plane': A Brown Shirt at War," *All Hands*, February 2002.

——, "The New Front Line," *All Hands*, February 2002.

Scott Johnson, "A Sleepless Night in the Cold," *Newsweek*, March 18, 2002.

Chris King, "Reservists Provide Experience for Expeditionary Squadron," *Officer*, June 2002.

Slobodan Lekic, "USS *Constellation* Crew Has Christmas a Day Early," *News Tribune*, December 25, 2002.

Beena Maharaj. "Portrait of a Citizen Airman," *The Officer*, May 2002.

James A. Marks, "Always Out Front," *Military Intelligence Professional Bulletin*, July–September 2002.

James C. McKinley Jr., "At Fort Drum, Family and Nuptial Worries," *New York Times*, September 22, 2001.

Robert Young Pelton, "The Legend of Heavy D & the Boys," *National Geographic Adventure*, March 2002.

Brian Perry, "It's a Beautiful Day: Arrival in Afghanistan," *The Officer*, June 2002.

Rick Reilly, "One Man's Super Bowl," *Sports Illustrated*, October 22, 2001.

Michael Ware, "On the Mop-Up Patrol," *Time*, March 25, 2002.

David Zucchino, "Chasing Phantoms Across Afghanistan," *Los Angeles Times*, December 29, 2002.

Internet Sources

ABC News, http://abcnews.go.com. "Anaconda Wraps Up," March 18, 2002.

Jeffrey Kofman, "The Tip of the Sword," October 12, 2001.

Andrew Morse, James Blue III, and Marni Harriman, "First Wave: The Soldiers' Story." March 22, 2002.

Steve Osunsami, "Under Pressure." July 29, 2002.

Air Force Link, www.af.mil.

Louis A. Arana-Barradas, "Airmen Making Calm Out of Chaos in Afghanistan," March 4, 2002.

Louis A. Arana-Barradas, "Bagram Troops Live in Austere Conditions," March 5, 2002.

Joe Bela, "AF Makes 1 Millionth Food Drop to Afghanistan," October 31, 2001.

Johnny Rhea, "Rumsfeld: War on Terrorism Not 'Easy, Quick Fix'," June 11, 2002.

Rina Amiri, "Comprehending the Quagmire," *Sojourner,* November 2001. www.sojourner.org.

Army Link News, www.dtic.mil.

Tom Bryant, "Spanish Hospital Under U.S. Flag in Afghanistan," February 7, 2002.

Christina Carde, "Afghan Army Graduates Fifth Battalion," January 9, 2003.

Reeba Critser, "Female MPs Join Infantry on Front Lines," October 30, 2002.

Rhonda M. Lawson, "Army Helps Open Three Afghan Schools," September 17, 2002.

Dave Marck, "Soldiers Teach in Afghan School," April 25, 2002.

Holly Plata, "Soldiers Bring Relief After Afghan Earthquake," April 9, 2002.

"Soldiers Helping Assess Afghan Infrastructure," January 11, 2002.

"Troops in Afghanistan Mark Holiday with Turkey, Minefield Marathon," December 3, 2002.

Chance Babin, "Bombs Away," *Citizen Airman,* June 2002. www.afrc.af.mil.

Martin Bentham and Adam Lusher, "'I Was Smiling: I Had Dropped My Bombs. They Hit,'" *Spectator,* October 21, 2001. www.telegraph.co.uk.

Osama bin Laden, "Jihad Against Jews and Crusaders," Jihad Unspun, February 23, 1998. www.jihadunspun.net.

Janet Boivin, "Men Make Their Mark in Military Nursing," *Nursing Spectrum,* November 1, 2002. http://community.nursingspectrum.com.

Michelle Boorstein, "American Soldiers Return from Afghanistan," *Corpus Christi Caller-Times,* April 4, 2002. www.caller.com.

———, "Soldiers Find Documents in Abandoned Al-Qaida Caves, Then Destroy the Hide-outs in Operation Mountain Lion," Efreedom News.com, April 6, 2002. www.efreedomnews.com.

Randy Britton, "Reserve Seabees Pave Way for Enduring Freedom in Afghanistan," *Naval Reservist News,* May 2002. www.navres.navy.mil.

David Buchbinder, "U.S. Troops Bring Little League to Afghanistan," *Christian Science Monitor,* August 19, 2002. www.csmonitor.com.

Gerald M. Carbone, "War on Terrorism—Bomb Squad," *Providence Journal,* October 28, 2001. http://multimedia.belointeractive.com.

CBS News, "Allied Troops Battle Afghan Rebels," January 28, 2003. www.cbs news.com.

———, "U.S. Troops Hurt in Ambush Flown Out," July 29, 2002. www.cbs news.com.

Joseph R. Chenelly, "Marines Land, Seize Desert Strip," Marine Corps Website, November 25, 2001. www.15meu.usmc.mil.

Philip Cheng and Laurie McBean, "Fly-through Data Generation of Afghanistan," *Earth Observation Magazine,* January 2002. www.eomonline.com.

CNN, www.cnn.com.

"Flyers: 'The Partnership of Nations Is Here to Help,'" October 18, 2001.

Nic Robertson and Kelly Wallace, "U.S. Rejects Taliban Offer to Try Bin Laden," October 7, 2001.

Martin Savidge, "A Man of No Caliber," February 19, 2002.

Martin Savidge, "A-Scrounging We Will Go," February 4, 2002.

Martin Savidge, "'Camp Candy Bar' and Thought for Food," February 8, 2002.

Martin Savidge, "Please Send Me a Dust-Buster," February 11, 2002.

Barbara Starr, "As Pentagon Burned, Plans for War Took Shape," September 6, 2002.

"U.S. Special Operations Troops in Commando Raid," October 22, 2001.

Company H, 4th Battalion, 7th Aviation Regiment, "Pilot Reports from Afghanistan," 2003. www.chinook-helicopter.com.

Thomas Michael Corcoran, "Soviet-era Gear Makes Life Easier for Servicemembers at Kandahar Airport," Marine Corps Website, December 31, 2001. www.usmc.mil.

Jennifer Dyer Cornelisson, "Just the Two of Us, Married Without Children," LIFElines Services Network, 2003. www.life lines2000.org.

Amanda Currier, "Airman Basic Amy Ting," Defend America, 2003. www.defend america.mil.

Defense Link, www.defenselink.mil.

Jim Garamone, "Rite of Passage," 2002.

Gerry J. Gilmore, "Rumsfeld Praises Civil Affairs' Work in Afghanistan," August 20, 2002.

Linda D. Kozaryn, "Army Reserve Duty Has 'Changed Forever,'" January 22, 2002.

Kathleen T. Rhem, "Civil Affairs Soldiers Assist Afghan Students, Leaders," October 18, 2002.

———, "Franks: A Leader Sure of his Mission and his Troops," January 5, 2002.

———, "Rumsfeld Believes U.S. Can Get Bin Laden," October 25, 2001.

———, "Soldiers Bring America's Pastime to Afghan Children," October 21, 2002.

Rudi Williams, "Reflections on Sept. 11, a Day of Terror," September 11, 2002.

Mike Eckel, "U.S. Veterinarians Are Working in Afghanistan," Associated Press, December 5, 2002. http://story.news.yahoo.com.

Andrew England, "Planes, Pilots and Carrier Crew Pushed to the Limit in Afghanistan Campaign," South Coast Today.com, December 15, 2001. www.s-t.com.

Bay Fang and Mark Mazzetti, "To the Death," *U.S. News & World Report*, March 18, 2002. www.usnews.com.

Fox News, "Military Couples Rush to Get Married," September 25, 2001. www.foxnews.com.

Frontline, www.pbs.org.
  "The Fall of Kandahar," 2002.
  "Friendly Fire," 2002.
  "Interview: Lt. Col David Fox," 2002.
  "Interview: U.S. Army Captain Jason Amerine," 2002.
  "Interview: U.S. Special Forces ODA 595," 2002.

Cal Fussman, "What I've Learned," *Esquire*, August 2002. www.esquire.com.

Barton Gelman, "Clinton's War on Terror," *Washington Post*, December 19, 2001. www.washingtonpost.com.

Joseph Giordono, "Deminers Slowly Clear Bagram Base," *European-Pacific Stars and Stripes*, June 30, 2002. www.roncoconsulting.com.

Susan B. Glasser, "Soldiers in Civilian Clothing," Associated Press, March 28, 2002. www.miraserve.com.

Craig Gordon, "Killed by Friendly Fire," *Newsday*, December 6, 2001. www.globalsecurity.org.

Chuck Goudie, "I-Team Exclusive: Chicagoans at the Front," *ABC News*, October 17, 2001. http://abclocal.go.com

Susan H. Greenberg, "Get Out of My Way," *MSNBC News*, October 29, 2001. www.msnbc.com.

Vic Harris, "Soldiers Find Water in Drought-Stricken Afghanistan," dcmilitary.com, January 25, 2002. www.dcmilitary.com.

Bob Haskell, "Guarding Terrorists," National Guard Association of the United States, February 2002. www.ngaus.org.

Robert Hayes, "Army Medic Supports U.S. Forces in Afghanistan," Hometown Link, 2002. http://hn.afnews.af.mil.

Seymour M. Hersh, "Escape and Evasion," *New Yorker*, November 12, 2001. www.newyorker.com.

Jefferson City News Tribune, "Marines Patrol Base, Review Security After Firefight During First Prisoner Transfer," January 11, 2002. http://newstribune.com.

Ron Kampeas, "Troops Adjust to Return Home," TeamCares, Inc., November 29, 2002. www.teamcares.org.

Stephen Kaufman, "Detainees, Guards Interact with Care at Camp X-Ray," U.S. Department of State, February 27, 2002. http://usinfo.state.gov.

———, "Military Doctors Attend to Detainee Maladies at Camp X-Ray," U.S. Department of State, February 28, 2002. http://usinfo.state.gov.

Kathleen Knox, "Afghanistan: Renewed Fighting Raises Question of U.S. 'Exit Strategy,'" *Radio Free Europe*, March 4, 2002. www.rferl.org.

Jim Kolbe, "Speech Before US Navy League and USS TUCSON 770 Club," United States Representative Jim Kolbe's Website, October 20, 2000. www.house.gov.

Rhonda M. Lawson, "Army Reserve PSYOP Soldiers Trade Toys for Guns in Kabul," United States Army Reserve, 2003. www.army.mil.

Gordon T. Lee, "Hard-Shelled, SOF-Centered: The Synergy of Might and Mind," *Rand Review,* Summer 2002. www.rand.org.

David Levinsky, "First Active-duty Airmen Move Out from McGuire," *Burlington County Times,* September 21, 2001. www.phillyburbs.com.

Tamara Lush, "Heaven in Time of War: 6700 Ribeyes," *St. Petersburg Times,* July 2, 2002. www.sptimes.com.

Rex McCarty, "Shoemaker Elementary Provides Gift Items to American Soldiers," *Scott County Virginia Star,* 2002. www.virginiastar.net.

Patrick D. McGowan, "Preface," Outside the Wire, no date. http://outsidethewire.net.

Stephan McGuire, "From Queens to Kandahar and Back: Answering the Call to Fight Terrorism," *Southeast Queens Press,* September 11, 2002. www.queenspress.com.

Robert McMahon, "UN: Security Council Condemns Taliban for Afghan Instability," *Radio Free Europe,* April 8, 2000. www.rferl.org.

April Middleton, "Soldier's Personal, Work Life Altered," *Kansas State Collegian,* September 11, 2002. www.kstatecollegian.com.

Matt Mientka, "Army Medics Aid Afghanistan," *U.S. Medicine,* October 2002. www.usmedicine.com.

Military Woman Home Page, "Army Meteorologist," August 30, 2002. www.militarywoman.org.

———, "Inflight Refueler Boom Operator," June 14, 2000. www.militarywoman.org.

Beth Miller, "For U.S. Troops, Daily Life Is Filled with Dangers," *News Journal,* April 17, 2002. www.delawareonline.com.

Milwaukee Journal Sentinel, "U.S. Soldiers Visit Afghan Orphans," July 28, 2002. www.jsonline.com.

Bryan Mitchell, "District Soldier Working to Make Life Better," U.S. Army Corps of Engineers, 2003. www.orn.usace.army.mil.

MSNBC News, "Massoud's Last Words," September 20, 2001. www.msnbc.com.

Kim Murphy and John Hendren, "Taliban Flees Kandahar, But Omar Escapes," Efreedom News.com, 2003. www.efreedomnews.com.

Steve Olafson, "Reservists, Troops Getting Affairs in Order," *Houston Chronicle,* September 15, 2001. www.chron.com.

Mark Oliva and Wayne Specht, "Fully Loaded, AC-130 Spectre Gunship Is Like an Airborne Tank," CheckPoint, October 21, 2001. www.checkpoint-online.ch.

Jon Ostendorff, "Families Eagerly Await 211th's Return," *Asheville Citizen-Times,* September 10, 2002. http://cgi.citizen-times.com.

Melissa Phillips, "Tech. Sgt. Keith Winchell," Defend America, September 18, 2002. www.defendamerica.mil.

Noelle Phillips, "In the Rear with the Gear," *Savannah Morning News,* April 21, 2002. www.savannahnow.com.

Allen Pizzey, "Troops Take a Break in Afghanistan," *CBS News,* December 25, 2002. www.cbsnews.com.

Kathleen T. Rhem, "SF Soldier Works with Army Reserve Medics," United States Army Reserve, 2002. www.army.mil.

———, "Special Forces Medic Reaches Out to Afghan People," Special Ops Medicine.com, 2002. www.specialopsmedicine.com.

Douglas Ritter, "Aerial Refueling," *Code One Magazine,* January 1993. www.codeone magazine.com.

Samaritan's Purse, "Samaritan's Purse Aid in Afghanistan Yields Grateful Hearts," July 20, 2002. www.samaritanspurse.org.

Rowan Scarborough, "'Special Ops' Gets OK to Initiate Its Own Missions," *Washington Times,* January 8, 2003. www.wash times.com.

Karin Schmidt, "Knight's Tale: A Call to Action for Nurse Reservist," *Nurse Week,* November 11, 2001. www.nurseweek.com.

J.A. Scordo, "Current Status," 26th Marine Expeditionary Unit, April 24, 2001. www.26meu.usmc.mil.

LaTorry Sidney, "Baseball Comes to Afghanistan," United States Central Command, August 24, 2002. www.centcom.mil.

Soldiers for the Truth Foundation, "Troops Latest Afghan Peril: Altitude," 2002. www.sftt.org.

Sydney Morning Herald, "Blue Christmas for Foreign Troops in Afghanistan," December 25, 2002. www.smh.com.au.

Cassie Tarpley, "Inside Camp Rhino," *Shelby Star,* April 8, 2002. www.shclbystar.com.

Third Age, Inc., "Preventing Disease Is Tough in Afghanistan," 2003. www.third age.com.

26th MEU, "Preparing to Go," November 28, 2001. http://192.156.19.109/mainelink/mcn2000.nsf.

Ann Scott Tyson, "US Finds Building Afghan Army Isn't Easy," *Christian Science Monitor,* March 13, 2002. www.csmonitor.com.

U.S. Army, www.goarmy.com.
"Recruit Profile: Basic Training," 2003.
"Soldier Profiles," 2003.
"Special Forces," 2003.

USA Today, "U.S. Forces Using the Net to Contact Home," May 7, 2002. www.usa today.com

Mike Vernon, "Daily Life in Kandahar," *CBC News,* May 20, 2002. http://cbc.ca.

Warships International Fleet Review, "USS Kitty Hawk Carries the War to the Terrorist," March 2003. www.warshipsifr.com.

The White House, www.whitehouse.gov.
"Address to a Joint Session of Congress and the American People," September 20, 2001.
"Excerpts from State of the Union Speech Regarding Defending Peace & Security at Home," January 28, 2003.
"President Directs Humanitarian Aid to Afghanistan," October 4, 2001.
"President: "We're Making Progress," October 1, 2001.

Judith Williams, "Psychologist Gets Underway Aboard Kitty Hawk," *Navy and Marine Corps Medical News,* October 17, 1996. www.chinfo.navy.mil.

Gregg Zoroya, "Commandos Fight Abroad Also a Hit at Home," *USA Today,* February 5, 2002. www.usatoday.com.

☆ Index ☆

★ Picture Credits ★

★ About the Author ★

Diane Yancey works as a freelance writer in the Pacific Northwest, where she has lived for more than twenty years. She writes nonfiction for middle-grade and high school readers and enjoys traveling and collecting old books. Some of her other books are *Life in War-Torn Bosnia, Strategic Battles* (Civil War), *Life of an American Soldier* (Vietnam War), and *Leaders and Generals* (War on Terrorism).